STORYTELLING
For The FUN Of It
A Handbook for Children

STORYTELLING
For The FUN Of It
A Handbook for Children

Vivian Dubrovin
Illustrated By Bobbi Shupe

STORYCRAFT
PUBLISHING

Masonville, CO   80541

Storycraft books are available at special discount for bulk purchases
for workshops, classes, promotions, or fund raising. Special editions
or book excerpts can also be created. For details contact:
Sales Director
Storycraft Publishing
P.O. Box 205
Masonville, CO 80541

Storycraft Publishing
P.O. Box 205
Masonville, CO 80541

Printed in the United States of America

Publisher's Cataloging in Publication
(Prepared by Quality Books Inc.)

Dubrovin, Vivian.
    Storytelling for the fun of it : a handbook for children / by
Vivian Dubrovin ; illustrated by Bobbi Shupe.
    p. cm.
    Includes bibliographical references and index.
    Preassigned LCCN: 93-93694.
    ISBN 0-9638339-0-1

    1. Storytelling.   I. Shupe, Bobbi, ill. II. Title.

LB1042.D83 1994   372.6'4
                              QBI93-22121

Other Books By
VIVIAN DUBROVIN

NONFICTION

Creative Word Processing
Guide To Alternative Education And Training
Paper Craft Ideas For The New Print Shop
Running A School Newspaper
The ABC's Of The New Print Shop
Write Your Own Story

FICTION

A Better Bit And Bridle
A Chance To Win
Baseball Just For Fun
Open The Gate
Rescue On Skis
The Magic Bowling Ball
The Track Trophy
Trailering Troubles

For all the storytellers in my family,

and all young storytellers everywhere.

ACKNOWLEDGMENTS

I would like to thank Ben McDonald for his help, advice, and support throughout this entire project.

I would also like to thank those who read the manuscript and contributed their suggestions: Norma Livo, Corinne Bergstrom, Linda White, Laurie Ihm, Bobbi Shupe, and Cathy Miller.

And many, many thanks to my entire family for all their patience and encouragement.

TABLE OF CONTENTS

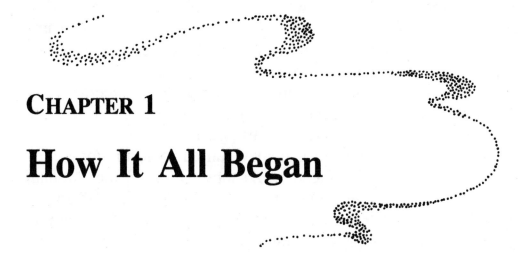

CHAPTER 1

How It All Began

A young man strode into the village square. He stopped in front of the big statue and glanced around at the merchants selling their wares. Then he whipped off his hat and plopped it on the ground in front of him to catch a coin or two. He picked up a small banjo and strummed a few loud chords. He waited for the townsfolk to gather around him. Then he began to play and sing:

"Gather 'round ye merry folk
and listen to tale or two..."

Long ago, before there was television, radio, newspapers, or even books, people got their news and entertainment from storytellers. Like this young man, they wandered from village to village and earned their living by telling tales. Some played an instrument and sang their stories. Some used magic tricks as they talked. Others depended on a simple prop or two to create a mood for their spellbinding dramas.

Then the printing press was invented and people preferred to read books, magazines, and newspapers. Later when radio came along, they wanted stories with sound effects. When television became popular, people wanted to see as well as hear stories.

Not so long ago, in the 1970's, many people realized that they were missing something. There was a magic in listening to a real live storyteller. So they began to tell stories again.

They had so much fun that they started to form storytelling clubs, hold festivals, and attend workshops. By 1993 the *National Directory of Storytelling*, published by NAPPS (The National Association for the Preservation and Perpetuation of Storytelling) listed 323 storytelling organizations and centers, 205 festivals and events, and 214 workshops and educational opportunities in the United States.

Because adults are having so much fun with storytelling, they are now encouraging young people to get in on this artform. Families are having story times. Teachers are developing storytelling programs. Churches and youth organizations are holding workshops for children.

Boys and girls are beginning to polish up their stories, trade and collect good telling tales, and look for every chance to be junior storytellers.

CHAPTER 2

Kids Tell Stories Today

★ **Where can kids tell stories?**
★ **Why are they doing it?**
★ **How can you get in on the fun?**

Since so many kids are discovering that storytelling is a lot of fun, it is an activity that is fast becoming very popular.

Where Kids Are Telling Stories

Kids are finding opportunities for storytelling in many places today. Some of those chances are just part of kids everyday activities.

Around Campfires

Did you ever sit around a campfire, roast hot dogs, and then toast marshmallows? When the sun went down and the stars came out, did you tell stories?

Long ago, in some cultures, one person was the storyteller. This person told the traditional tales that had been handed down from generation to generation. Today, everyone around a campfire may share a tale. Sometimes they are funny stories. Other times they are scary ghost stories.

At Slumber Parties

While many kids at slumber parties still watch videos, others are turning to storytellers. Sometimes the storytellers are neighborhood adults or someone's older brother or sister. But often the storyteller is just one of the guests, a classmate or friends, who likes to tell stories and is willing to create a ghost just for your special occasion.

In Classroom Projects

Your first experience with storytelling may be during a project in your classroom at school.

In Joshua'a fifth grade literature class, a local storyteller told some legends. She then helped the students find stories to tell at a storytelling performance for their parents.

In Karla's sixth grade class, some boys and girls learned stories to tell to kindergarten and first grade children. After telling their stories at their school, they visited other schools.

Todd's fourth grade class told stories about their town as part of their study of local history. A storyteller came to their classroom dressed as one of the town's famous pioneers and told about homesteading, wagon trains, and why the railroad runs through the south of their town. Then the children chose historical characters or events and created their own stories. They had so much fun, they put on a

6

storytelling concert for the third graders to get them interested in studying local history next year.

In Public Library Programs

You might find a storytelling workshop at your public library. Like school projects, library programs often begin with a professional storyteller. You will then get to work with the storyteller to find and develop your own story.

Public libraries have many legends, fairy tales, folk tales, and other stories. Library programs will encourage you to read the books that they have.

In Religious Programs

You might have a chance to tell stories during your religious school classes, especially at holidays.

Some kids are retelling the old stories just as they have been handed down, while others are creating contemporary stories based on the story theme in an attempt to understand or explain their beliefs.

Arnie's vacation Bible school class devoted two weeks to story-telling. They made puppets and crafts to go with their stories. On the last day they presented a program for the church.

During Vacations and Car Pool Rides

On long vacation rides, many families play games or tell stories in the car to pass the time. Now families that began storytelling during long trips are also playing story-games and telling mini-tales during car pool rides. Sometimes they make up stories that need to be continued during the next ride. It makes car pooling a lot more fun!

At Family Gatherings

After a holiday meal some families gather on a front porch or around a fireplace to share family history.

Roberto's father always tells about the escape to this country. Dan's dad likes to tell old war stories. Carolee says she gets the best stories from her parents and grandparents during family chores or other activities. However, she admits, that sometimes the stories are the "when I was your age" kind, and are *not* meant to be entertaining.

While Babysitting

While many babysitters happily read a bedtime story to their charges, other young people are discovering that special stories can be the key to hassle free sitting. Getting kids to do the things they need to do, picking up toys, eating their meals, or going to bed, is much easier accompanied by the right story.

Debbie says she was forced into creative storytelling during a violent thunderstorm when she was trying to convince two terrified preschoolers not to be afraid of the lightning. She made up a story about cloud children with new flashlights.

Babysitters who make up their own stories for kids when they need them are now sharing their tales with friends and collecting "sitter tales."

At Festivals

Some storytelling festivals now include special workshops for kids who want to learn how to tell stories. Many school, library, or youth group workshops may hold a festival or at the end of their storytelling project.

Why Kids Tell Stories

Kids are telling stories for the fun of it. Even shy kids are discovering that there is a certain joy when everyone in a classroom, or large auditorium is glued to your every word. On the other hand, boys and girls who love to be in the spotlight every chance they can get are finding that this is really an activity that is tailor made for them.

It's fun to make a group of people laugh because you told a joke or a funny story. And it's a different kind of fun to make their eyes grow wide or have them jump in their chairs because you scared them. It's also fun to tell a nice warm story that makes people think, remember, or learn something new.

Some kids like the sharing, telling and listening, to stories about their hobbies and interests. Other kids enjoy the friends they make when they go to storytelling festivals and parties. And a few kids even enjoy the understanding and learning they gather from the stories.

Whatever the reason that gets kids to start storytelling, it's the special magic that holds them, makes them want to continue, and turns them into avid storytellers.

How You Can Join the Fun

Helping you join in the storytelling fun is what this book is all about. It's full of ideas, tips, and resources to get you started. It will:

> ☺ Help you find stories to tell
> with examples of stories
> ideas for adapting old stories
> ideas for creating new ones

☺ Give resources
    books of stories
    video and audio tapes of storytellers
☺ Help you gather information
    by playing detective to uncover local history
    by interviewing family members or neighbors
☺ Give you tips and techniques
    for learning a story
    for practicing a story
    for telling stories
    for using costumes, props, and puppets
☺ Help you create storytelling opportunities
    by holding a storytelling party
    by starting a storytelling club
    by having a storytelling festival

Look for storytelling opportunities wherever you can find them. And join in the fun!

PART II
How To Find Stories To Tell

CHAPTER 3

Three Magic Tips

★ **How do you choose a story to tell?**
★ **Why is the audience important?**
★ **How do you know if a story is right for you?**

You will read many stories before you choose the one you want. While you are reading, look for a short story that can be told in ten minutes or less. Look for a simple plot or main idea that has a beginning, middle, and ending. The story you choose to tell should not be too complicated.

Here are three magic tips for choosing a story to tell:

1. Find a story your audience will like.

Where will you tell your story? Who will listen to it? What do they want to hear? How many people will be in the audience?

2. Know *why* you are telling the story.

Do you want to make someone laugh? Or cry? Do you want to frighten your audience? Or just entertain them? Maybe your story is an explanation to help your audience understand something. Or it may be educational to teach history or a new idea.

3. Find a story you like.

You must *really* enjoy the story you plan to tell, because you will be working with it for a long time.

Although the third tip is very important, the first and second ones will be most helpful in selecting a story. Will your audience be a few of your friends at a slumber party, 50 classmates at school, or 200 parents in an auditorium?

Because your audience is so important in story selection, think about some places where you could tell stories--campouts, slumber parties, classrooms programs, library projects, church and religious programs, car pool rides, family storytelling, babysitter storytime, and storytelling clubs. Read Chapters 4 through 11 to find out how to select the best story for each audience.

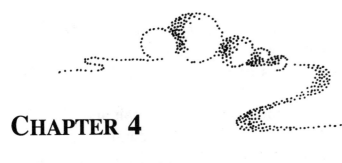

CHAPTER 4

At Campouts

★ **How long will you be camping out?**
★ **Who is camping with you?**
★ **What stories are best for a campout?**

Whether you are going to camp for one overnight or stay a week or two, you will have a campfire and hopefully a campfire storytime.

It's fun to sit under the stars and listen to stories, but it's even more fun to tell them.

What kind of stories do you tell at a campout?

Some camps have their own legends or history. If you have been to this place before, you could share these stories with first time visitors.

If you are camping in a national, state or local park, you might want to tell a nature story. There are many legends about why plants are this color, that shape, or why their leaves whisper in the wind.

There are animal legends about how bear lost his tail, how skunk got his stripe, and the great race between rabbit and turtle.

And, there are scary stories of ghosts, monsters, and strange creatures of the night.

One of Cindy's favorite nature stories is "Rabbit and The Trail Signs." She first heard it on an overnight. Her scouting group was learning how to mark and follow a trail. Some children planned to lay a trail, and other children had agreed to try to follow it. At storytime the night before the trail hike, the leader told this story. When Cindy tells it at campouts now, she asks everyone to pick up twelve stones to help with the story.

Rabbit and The Trail Signs

Rabbit had been watching the campers that came to State Park for years. Every time he learned something new. His favorite thing was watching children lay and follow trail signs.

Rabbit's second most favorite thing was playing tricks on the squirrel family that lived in the big oak tree.

Mother squirrel always worried about her babies. The two baby squirrels would believe almost anything Rabbit told them. And Father Squirrel seldom understood anything Rabbit said.

So, one day when Rabbit thought he had learned a few trail signs, he decided to play a game with the squirrel family. He gathered them together under the big oak tree and explained the rules that he had learned from the children.

16

"Whenever you come to a spot where two paths cross, place a trail sign to tell me which way to go." Rabbit put three acorns on the ground, two in a row, and one on the right side. "This," said Rabbit, "means turn to the right."

(Cindy put three stones on the ground in this pattern **:•** *and asked everyone in the audience to do the same with three of their stones.)*

"If I put two acorns in a row and one on the left side," said Rabbit, "it means you should turn left."

(Cindy put three stones in this pattern **•:** *and asked her audience to do the same with three stones.)*

"Then," said Rabbit, "if you see only two acorns in a row, that means to go straight ahead."

(Cindy placed only two stones in a vertical line **:** *and asked her audience to do the same with two stones.)*

Then, because Rabbit knew that Father Squirrel was slow and Mother Squirrel wasn't paying attention, he reviewed the instructions.

(Cindy reviews the instructions with her audience.)

Rabbit tells Squirrel family to count to 10 to give him time to get started. Then follow him. And Rabbit runs down the park trail.

When Rabbit comes to the first crosspath, he puts three acorns in the middle of the trail like this •• which means what?

(Cindy lets her audience answer.)

Then Rabbit runs down the right path until he comes to another cross path. In the middle he places three acorns like this •• which means what?

(Cindy let's her audience answer again.)

Then Rabbit runs down the left path until he comes to another cross path. In the middle of the trail he puts two acorns in a vertical line like this • and he runs straight ahead.

But Rabbit has saved a secret sign for last. He chuckles as he thinks of Mother Squirrel not paying attention and Father Squirrel not understanding. And then he lays out his secret sign like this ••••

(Cindy asks her audience to use their last four stones for the secret sign.)

Then Rabbit hides behind a bush to wait for the Squirrel family and watch what they do. Rabbit thinks that his secret sign means END OF THE TRAIL, and he plans to share his lunch of leftover acorns with the squirrels when they arrive.

18

When the Squirrel family starts down the park trail, Mother Squirrel leads the way. When she comes to the first sign **:•** she remembers and says,

(Cindy lets her audience answer.)

Baby Boy Squirrel leads the way to the next marker **•:** and he remembers that it means,

(Cindy lets her audience answer.)

Baby Girl Squirrel leads the way to the next marker **:** and she remembers that it means,

(Cindy lets her audience answer.)

But now it is Father Squirrel's turn and he leads the way. Except, he spots the marker before he gets there. It's a new sign. It's different and he's afraid.

"Danger!" he yells. "Rabbit is warning us of danger." He turns around. "Run back! Quick!"

The Squirrel Family runs back down the path.

"Quickly! Quickly!" Mother Squirrel tells her babies. Gather the acorns as we leave so nobody else runs into danger." And she scoops up the trail sign that says straight ahead.

(Cindy picks up those two stones and asks the audience to do the same.)

They run to the next marker and Baby Girl picks up the acorns that say turn left.

(Cindy picks up those three stones and asks the audience to do the same.)

They run to the last marker, and Baby Boy picks up the acorns that say go right.

(Cindy picks up those three stones and asks the audience to do the same.)

They run to the old oak tree and hide the acorns.

Now, Rabbit, back at the bush, jumps up and tries to stop the squirrels. But since they have taken the acorns, he gets lost.

So, even today, if you see a rabbit in the park, it will be running around looking for something. If you see a squirrel, it will be gathering and hiding acorns. And, if you mark a path in the park, use stones *(Cindy holds up some of the stones)* and never use acorns.

There are many stories where a "trickster character" tries to play jokes on people or other animals. Coyote tales from the southwest American Indian tribes are quite popular. The wee folk of

Ireland, the leprechauns and fairies, also like to play tricks.

You can use trickster tales just as you find them or create new stories by changing the characters. Instead of a coyote, make him a witch, a monster or a creature from outer space. You can change the other characters, too. Or, you can change the setting. Have the story take place in a big city, on a boat, or on another planet.

Changing parts of old stories is the easiest way to create new ones. Use one story as the pattern for a new one.

You can change ghost stories the same way. For example, one popular ghost story pattern is the appearance of someone who has died. It usually starts with your hero character driving or walking at night and meeting a stranger. The stranger is very friendly and often needs help. The hero helps the stranger who then leaves. Later the hero finds something the stranger left or lost and tries to return it only to discover that the stranger has been dead for many years.

Elly used this pattern for her Canyon Camper story.

The Canyon Camper

My little brother thought the signs were silly. I know he did.

We were driving down the canyon road, through the narrows. The rock walls rose higher than any city building on both sides of the road. In some places there was only room for the road and the creek that ran beside it.

Then the canyon became a little wider and there was grass on the other side of the creek and a house and cabins.

21

"Is that it?" asked my mother. "Help us look for the Canyon Cabins, Elly. We should be almost there."

I looked for signs to identify the tourist lodges we were passing. But Benjie was fascinated with the green road signs that said, In Case Of Flood, Climb To Safety.

"How silly," my little brother said. "What else would you do?"

We ignored him because we spotted the Canyon Cabins.

After supper Benjie and I went to the creek to throw stones into the water.

"There's hardly any water," he said, plopping a big rock into the shallow creek.

I hopped from one large rock to another until I was out in the middle of the creek. I picked up a pretty pink stone and hopped back.

Benjie picked up a sparkling rock. We took our stones back to show Mom and Dad. They were sitting outside our cabin talking to some of the other guests. Two more people joined us, a girl a little older than me and a man older than my dad. I remember the man because he was wearing a red-and-black-checkered jacket and an orange hunting hat. It was a cool night but not that cold. I especially remember him because he got so mad when Benjie talked again about the silly safety signs.

The man told us about a big flood. He said the river—he called this creek a river—was as high as a twisted pine tree way up on the hill. He said the water came fast that night. He said it washed out all the buildings and even the road.

He took off his hat and ran his fingers through his stringy brown hair. His face still looked mad and he talked on and on about that terrible night of the big flood.

22

I was glad when Mom said it was time for bed, because the flood stories were getting pretty scary. I lay in bed and wondered about that little creek and this man's wall of water.

The next morning, as we were getting ready to leave, I saw the man's orange hunting hat still on the ground beside the chair where he was sitting. Dad told me to take it to the office when we left.

My family waited in the car while I went into the office. I put the hat on the counter and tried to describe the man to the lady behind the desk.

Her face looked very strange. She motioned to the wall behind me, to a picture on the wall, a newspaper picture.

"Yeah, that's him," I said.

"That's ol' Jake Swenson. He used to own this place. Drowned in the big flood 20 years ago today. He tried to get all the guests to climb to safety, but he didn't climb fast enough himself. He and his young daughter died that night.

Use this pattern to create a scary ghost story for your next campout, especially if you are camping beside a mountain stream.

For Further Reading

Tales about how animals got the way they are can be found in collections of legends. These books are in the nonfiction section of your library.

Stories about animals, such as dogs and cats, will be in the fiction section.

Check the library computer or card catalog. You will find a list of both fiction and nonfiction. Some books you can look for are:

A Treasury of Animal Stories, by Linda Yeatman, Simon and Schuster, 1982.
Animal Folk Tales, by Barbara Ker Wilson, Grosset and Dunlop, 1983.
The Legend of the Bluebonnet, by Tomie de Paola, Putnam, 1983.
Why the Possum's Tail Is Bare and other North American Indian Nature Tales, by James E. Connally, Stemmer House, 1985.

Scary stories will be found in the fiction section of your library under the author's last name. Some libraries put stickers on the fiction books to help you find the kind you are looking for. Look for stickers that say *Horror* or *Halloween*. Some collections of scary stories are:

Thirty Chilling Tales Short and Shivery, by Robert D. San Souci, Doubleday, 1987.
Scary Stories for Sleep-overs, by R.C. Welch, Price, Stern, Sloan, 1991.
Scary Stories to Tell in the Dark, by Alvin Schwartz, Harper & Row, 1981.
Whistle in the Graveyard: Folktales to Chill Your Bones, by Maria Leach, Viking, 1974.

24

Chapter 5

At Slumber Parties

★ **How do you tell group stories?**
★ **What are string stories?**
★ **How do you make a demonstration part of a story?**

Slumber parties are great places to tell group stories, string stories, or demonstration stories. Because slumber party guests probably know each other, they can have a lot of fun creating a story together. Since the group is small and can gather around the storyteller, everyone can see a demonstration.

Group Stories

In group stories, each person tells part of the story. One person might create the main character. Another tells what that character wants. A third person might describe the scene.

To get the story going, write directions on small pieces of paper or cards to tell each person what to do. Number the cards so the storytellers will know whose turn it is. The storytellers can be serious or silly, and the stories are meant to be funny.

On the next pages, there are some ideas for story directions. You can photocopy this page and cut on the lines. Use the paper pieces or paste them onto index cards. If there are only a few people, give each person two or three cards. If there are many guests, you can make up extras.

As each person uses his card, he places it in the story pile. The story is over when all the cards are used up. Wild card players may use their cards at any time but must use them before card #12 has been placed in the story pile.

String Stories

Have you ever taken a loop of string and created string figures such as a cat's cradle? Many storytellers work with strings while they are telling stories. Sometimes they create just one figure. Sometimes they turn one into another. But, sometimes they keep changing the creations as they tell the story.

If you like to work with strings, and are good at it, you may want to tell string stories. There are many books that can help you learn them. One book is *The Story Vine*, by Anne Pellowski (Collier Books, 1984).

Story Cards For Group Story

1 **The Main** **Character is**	**2** **The Setting** **is**	**3** **The Time** **is**
4 **Other People** **are**	**5** **The Main** **Character wants**	**6** **First thing the** **Main Character** **does**
7 **What happens to** **the Main** **Character**	**8** **What does** **Main Character** **do now?**	**9** **What happens to** **the Main** **Character**
10 **How Main** **Character tries to** **fix things**	**11** **Does it solve** **everything?**	**12** **How does the** **story end?**

27

Wild Card Add Another Character	***Wild Card*** Add Something To The Scene	***Wild Card*** Add A Stinky Smell
Wild Card Add A Bitter Taste	***Wild Card*** Add A Loud Sound	***Wild Card*** Add A Nice Smell
Wild Card Add A Pleasant Taste	***Wild Card*** Add A Soft Sound	***Wild Card*** Add An Animal
Wild Card Add A Machine	***Wild Card*** Add Some Food	***Wild Card*** Add A Plant

Craft Demonstrations

If there is a craft you know how to do, you might want to demonstrate how to do it while you tell the story. At a slumber party you could show everyone else how to make their own crafts.

For example, you could demonstrate how to make a cornhusk doll, or how to cut snowflake designs, or how to create shell animals or pom pom critters.

Mindy told the story of The Magic Dream Doll at a slumber party while demonstrating how to make a 4-inch yarn doll. Using the instructions at the end of this chapter, she created a sample.

Read the story once to enjoy it. Then read it a second time to figure out how Mindy demonstrated the craft. She did not finish the sample until the end of the story.

The Magic Dream Doll

Maria's grandmother was dying. Her hands trembled as she struggled to open the skein of yarn. Her fingers fumbled to find the loose end. Hands that once had so skillfully worked knitting needles and weaving looms now could barely pull yarn from a skein.

Maria carefully took the skein in her hands and helped to free the yarn.

"I want to show you how to make a Dream Doll," her grandmother said softly. "I want you to know the magic."

Maria continued to pull yarn from the skein as her grandmother slowly wound it around the length of a small rectangular piece of cardboard.

29

"This Dream Doll is very special," her grandmother said. She paused and looked at Maria. "We have talked, told stories, shared things we like and would like to have. We have dreamed together."

Maria's grandmother stopped winding and cut the yarn. She tied one end and carefully slipped the yarn off the cardboard. About an inch from the end, she tied the yarn together again.

Maria watched carefully. The yarn looked like the tassels she and her grandmother had once made for a shawl.

Her grandmother picked up the cardboard again and began winding yarn around the width. "After I am gone," she said, "I want you to carry this Dream Doll with you to remember me."

Maria pulled out more yarn. "It will not be like you," she said.

"No," said her grandmother gently, "but it will listen to your stories. It will always listen to your dreams." She slipped the yarn off the cardboard. "There is a magic that happens when you tell your dreams to a Dream Doll." Grandmother put the doll's arms in place.

"Magic?" asked Maria.

"Magic!" said Grandmother. "When you tell your dreams to a Dream Doll, they come true, they really happen."

"Oh, that's silly," said Maria. "That little yarn doll can't make my dreams come true."

"Try it," Grandmother said. "One day, you will see." Grandmother gave her the doll. "Put it in your pocket. Keep it with you."

Maria put the doll in her pocket.

After her grandmother died, Maria always wore clothes with pockets. She carried the Dream Doll in her jeans pocket. She carried it in her shirt pocket. When the weather was cold, she put it in her coat pocket.

When she felt lonely, she would slip her hand into her pocket and touch the little yarn doll. Then she would feel better. Perhaps, she thought, it was a tiny bit of magic. But, she could never talk to the doll, tell it stories, or share her dreams. That, she thought, was silly.

Maria missed her grandmother very much. She missed the advice her grandmother always had for problems. She missed the stories they told each other about things that happened during the day. But, most of all she missed sharing her dreams, the dreams about what she wanted to do, what she wanted to be.

One day, when Maria was feeling especially lonely, she reached into her coat pocket and touched the little doll. The tiny bit of magic flowed through her. She pulled the doll out of her pocket and held it in her hands. But she could not talk to it or tell it her dreams. That, she thought, was silly.

As her birthday approached, Maria felt worse and worse. Her birthday had always been important. Her grandmother had always planned something special.

Maria remembered last year's birthday and one long ago. She remembered things that she and her grandmother had planned for this year. And now those things would never happen.

Days passed and the birthday came closer. Nothing happened. Nobody seemed to remember.

The day before her birthday, Maria ran all the way home from school. She pushed open the big front door and ran into the empty kitchen. She sat down in a chair, pulled the Dream Doll out of her pocket and placed it on the table.

She began to cry. She told the Dream Doll about the best birthday she had ever had. Then she told the Dream Doll what she and her grandmother had been planning for this year and what she was really hoping would happen. She put her head on the table and cried and cried. She cried so hard she got the little doll all wet with tears.

The next day she had the best birthday. It became her favorite birthday. She got everything she had wanted.

She still carries the little doll in her pocket every day. Every night she takes it out and tells it about her problems. She tells it stories about what happened that day. Then she tells it her dreams.

So, keep a Dream Doll in your pocket and remember, every night, to tell it your dreams. Try it, you'll see."

After finishing the story, Mindy gave each girl at the slumber party some yarn and a 3-inch x 4-inch piece of cardboard. They all shared one pair of scissors. As the guests each created their own Dream Doll, they discussed Mindy's story.

"That *is* silly," said Sue. "A yarn doll can't make your dreams come true, can it Mindy?"

Mindy just shrugged and said, "Try it, you'll see."

Try Mindy's story and demonstration at your next party.

32

How To Make A Dream Doll

To make a Dream Doll you will need:

Scissors

A 3-inch x 4-inch piece of cardboard (Any cardboard will do. You can cut it out of an old cereal box.)

4-ply knitting yarn (Thin yarn works best for this small size yarn doll. Do not use a bulky yarn.)

Cut five 6-inch pieces of yarn for tying. Put aside until needed.

Wind yarn 20 times around the four-inch length of the cardboard. Cut the end of the yarn.

With a 6-inch piece of yarn, tie the strands together at one edge of the cardboard. This will be the top of the doll's head. Gently slip the yarn off the cardboard. With another 6-inch piece of yarn, make the head by tying all strands together about 1-inch from the first tie. This is the doll body. Set it aside.

Now make the doll's arms by winding yarn 10 times around the three-inch width of the cardboard. Cut the end of the yarn.

Slip the yarn off the cardboard. Hold all strands together. (You may want someone to hold the strands while you tie them.)

Make hands by tying all arm strands together ½-inch from each end. Use one piece of 6-inch yarn for each hand.

33

Pick up the doll body. Divide the yarn strands beneath the head and insert the arms between them. Using the last 6-inch piece of yarn, tie all strands together just below the arms to hold them in place.

If you want your Dream Doll wearing a skirt, cut the loops. The doll will look like a small tassel.

If you want your Dream Doll wearing pants, divide the remaining strands in half to make legs. Cut two more 6-inch pieces of yarn and make feet by tying each leg ½-inch from the end.

For Further Reading

You can find some ideas for craft demonstrations in the non-fiction section of your library on shelves marked 745. You can also find some very good ideas by visiting your local craft and fabric stores and looking for booklets and leaflets on how to make crafts.

Here are some examples of the kind of books you might find:

Crafts From Recyclables, edited by Coleen Van Blaricom, Boyds Mills Press, 1992.

Incredibly Awesome Crafts For Kids, Better Homes and Gardens Books, 1992.

Paper Cutting Stories A to Z, by Valerie Marsh, Alleyside Press, 1993.

Paper Stories, by Jean Stangl, Fearon Teacher Aids, 1984.

Pom-Pom Puppets, Stories, & Stages, by Marj Hart and Walt Shelly, Fearon Teacher Aids, 1989.

The Family Storytelling Handbook, by Anne Pellowski, Macmillan, 1987.

The Story Vine, by Anne Pellowski, Collier Books, 1984.

CHAPTER 6

For Classroom Programs

★ **Can you uncover a secret story about your town?**
★ **Is there a story in your math book?**
★ **How can mixing myth and science make a story?**

Not all storyteller stories are make believe. Some of them are true stories.

In your classroom projects you may have an chance to explore true stories. Many school storytelling programs focus on local history, math, or science. Some school projects have holiday themes.

Local History

Few communities are lucky enough to have books written about them. In many towns, counties, and states, most local history is still in the stories people tell. Finding these stories is a little like a treasure hunt. You may have to play detective to search out the facts and uncover secrets that have been hidden for a long time.

How do you know where to begin? Remember those three tips for selecting a story in Chapter 3? Remember the first one? Here is a time when YOU come first. What do YOU want to learn about?

You might want to know more about one of the town's founding fathers or the state's first governor. Why is your town where it is? Is there a park or monument? How and why did it get there? Is there a railroad or airport? Was there a fight over where it was built?

Ideas For Local History Stories

Who started the town newspaper and why?
Why is the county or state capitol where it is?
What are the native animals? Were there ever others?
How did first farmers or ranchers get started?
Why did first businesses come to town?
Why is your town where it is and not somewhere else?
Where was the first school and who was its first teacher?
Was there a great flood, fire, drought in your area?
How did the first trains, harbor, airport get there?
Who built the first hospital and why?
How did your town get it's name?
How did the rivers or parks get their name?
Why is there a city or state park? Or university?
Who were the first people who lived in your area?

Do you or any of your friends have grandparents that can remember how things were in this town when they were your age? Talk to them. Ask questions.

Old newspapers are good places to find stories about things that happened long ago. Public libraries usually have collections of old newspapers. They may be kept on film.

Be careful not to just collect a lot of facts. While that can be very interesting, it is not a story.

To make it a good story, look for the reason *why* something happened. *Why* was the shopping center built on McGregor's cornfield and not in Mr. Jones's apple orchard? Is there a story behind *why* the dam broke and flooded the valley? Is there a story behind the story?

Math Stories

You can create some good stories from the math problems in your workbooks. You know those story problems. "If John had a dollar and went to the store for a loaf of bread that cost 79 cents, how much change did he get?

Surely you can make this problem more interesting. Why did John need bread? What were his choices? If he bought the cheaper one, could he also get a candy bar? Could he trade the candy bar?

Take this problem as an example.

> A car travels 65 miles per hour for 15 miles
> on a highway, then travels 45 miles per hour
> for 10 miles on an access road, then 35
> miles per hour for 5 miles through town.
> How long will it take to make the trip?

Does it sound like your mom or dad asking how long it will take to drive you to a soccer game or a youth group function in a nearby town? Pretend it is.

You can begin to turn this math problem into a story by asking some questions. Who is driving? Where is that person going? Why is he making the trip?

Continue to brainstorm ideas about this drive. Is it a simple trip between two places or a detour? Why is there a detour? Do you pick up other people on the way? What is the weather today? What kind of traffic do you meet? Do you pass an accident? Does anyone in the car get sick?

When you have asked all the questions you can imagine, begin to assemble those ideas into some sort of order. Begin to put those ideas into a story form. You could begin this story this way.

Driving To The Soccer Game

I needed a ride to the soccer game in Bentsville. It wasn't far, just 15 miles on the highway, then 10 miles into town, and 5 miles to the junior high school. Mom couldn't take me because she was driving my little sister to a drama rehearsal. Dad had to see a client but would meet me at the game and bring me home. So Josh Hansen's dad said he would drive us both. Josh lives on the other side of our town. His dad wanted to allow a little extra time because there was a detour, a bridge out, on the access road.

Try to finish the story. When other kids find out Mr. Hansen is driving, do they all need a ride? Does he borrow a van and then rent a bus? Or does something happen at the detour? Does Josh get sick and need to be rushed to a hospital with a police escort? Think of as many things as you can to make this a very eventful ride.

You could end your story with a comment such as this.

Next week our team plays in Weston and I need a ride. Do you know anyone going that way?

Open your math book. Find a story problem. Start expanding it. Can you turn it into a funny tale?

Science Stories

Exploring why things happen can produce some good stories. Why does ice melt? What if, one day, for some reason, you had to keep a block of ice from melting. Why would it be necessary and how would you do it?

There are also some very good stories about how things were invented or discovered. Who invented the first car, train, bicycle? Why? Who discovered the North Pole? How?

Sometimes, you can create interesting stories by combining ancient myths with modern scientific theory. Take an old legend about what causes thunder or lightning and combine it with what really creates this phenomenon.

39

Reggie combined his science project with a literature assignment to create a storytelling story of Butterfly People.

The Butterfly People

I was doing a science project when I first saw them. I was studying the butterflies in my grandmother's garden.

Mom says I just got my school projects all tangled up. I was also studying tales of leprechauns, brownies, and gnomes for a storytelling program in my reading class.

My grandfather says I just have a wild imagination. And he was there, mowing the grass, at the very same time.

Anyway, this is how it happened. My grandmother had given me this jar, this one right here, to catch butterflies so I could look at them closer. I had to promise to let them go when I was through.

My grandfather didn't think I needed to catch them at all. He said I should just sit very still and watch.

So, I was sitting there in my grandmother's garden. It was a warm summer day and no wind at all. Three little orange and black butterflies were flying around, landing on one flower after another and never stopping anyplace.

Maybe that's why I first noticed this special one. It landed in the pansies and stayed for awhile, as if it were resting. Then it flew across the patio to a pot of geraniums. From there, it flew to the window box of petunias.

It had the most gorgeous wings of purple, yellow, white and black. I knew that I had to capture this one and take a closer look.

So, I took this jar in my left hand, like this, and the lid in my right hand, like this, and I crept to that window box. The butterfly didn't see me. It was busy doing something.

I had read in a science book how hummingbirds look for nectar in flowers and how bees pollinate the blossoms. I wondered if this butterfly was looking for nectar or pollinating the petunias. Whatever it was doing, it didn't see me.

I crept closer and closer. Then, in one quick move, I scooped the jar and snapped the lid, like this. And I had it!

It fluttered around frantically at first. Then it stood on the bottom of the jar, looked at me, and stamped its foot.

Was I surprised! I leaned close, with my eye right up to the jar, like this, and studied the tiny creature. t wasn't a butterfly at all. It was a tiny person with big beautiful wings and it was very angry.

I hollered for Grandfather to come see, but the lawnmower was so loud he couldn't hear me. He just waved from across the yard and went on mowing.

The Butterfly Person stopped stamping its foot and sat in the middle of the bottom of the jar. I opened the jar a tiny turn and heard a teeny voice scream, "Let me out of here! How can I do my work when I'm trapped?"

"Work?" I spoke very softly.

"My story work," it screamed again.

"Story work?" I asked.

It smiled. Then it kinda glowed. "Of course," it said slyly. "Butterfly People carry stories from one kind of flower to another."

"Were you carrying stories from the pansies to the geraniums?" I asked.

"The geraniums were very happy to hear my pansy story and gave me a good geranium one in return, which I was taking to the petunias when I was so rudely interrupted."

I thought it was a wonderful idea to carry stories from one place to another.

"Now," said the Butterfly Person, "if you let me out of this jar, I'll tell you a good story about Butterfly People."

I wanted to learn more about these fascinating little creatures, so I lifted the lid of the jar. The Butterfly Person quickly flew out of the jar and over to a rose bush.

I knew I'd been had. It just wanted me to release it. I watched it fly from the white rose bush to the red roses to the yellow ones. I sat very still and watched the Butterfly Person.

It did not fly out of the garden, but flew to my shoulder. It stood close to my ear and shouted. "Butterfly People not only carry stories from one kind of flower to another, but from garden to garden," it said. "Butterfly People travel from Mexico to Canada, north in the spring, and south in the fall. I must go now, but I will be back."

It flew around my head to my other shoulder and shouted in that ear. "You may tell your friends about the Butterfly People. Tell them to watch for us when we travel through. Perhaps one will stand on their shoulder and tell them a flower story." The Butterfly Person flew away.

I didn't believe it, of course. Mexico to Canada, indeed!

The next day in science class everyone reported on their observations of butterflies. Someone told about Monarch butterflies and how they migrate.

42

I didn't tell about my experience then. But if you ever study butterflies in your science class, look closely and you may find a Butterfly Person, and it might shout a story in your ear.

Holiday Stories

How did Groundhog Day get started? What's the real history of Thanksgiving Day? What are the legends behind May Day?

If everyone in your class looked for stories about one holiday, you could have a good storytelling party to celebrate that holiday.

Don't just look at the most popular holidays. Look for the lesser known ones. Many new holidays appear every year. What about Grandparent's Day or Secretary's Day?

Cultural Projects

Many classrooms have cultural projects. You might study the legends from your own or another culture. Sharing stories from around the world is a lot of fun. You might want to put on a cultural festival to share your stories with others. See Chapter 20 for ideas on putting on a festival.

For Further Reading

There are many interesting holiday stories. Here are a few to get you started.

By the Light of the Halloween Moon, by Caroline Stutson, Morrow, 1993.
First Thanksgiving, by Jean Craighead George, Putnam, 1993.
Oh, What a Thanksgiving!, by Steven Kroll, Scholastic, 1988.

Hanukkah!, by Roni Schotter, Little, Brown & Company, 1990.

The Jolly Christmas Postman, by Janet & Allan Ahlberg, Little, Brown & Company, 1991.

Mr Willowby's Christmas Tree, by Robert Barry, McGraw-Hill, 1963.

The Mother's Day Mice, by Eve Bunting, Clarion Books, 1986.

A Perfect Father's Day, by Eve Bunting, Clarion Books, 1991.

Clever Tom and the Leprechaun, by Linda Shute, Lothrop, Lee & Shepard, 1988.

There are collections of folk tales from almost every culture. Here are two collections that include tales from many lands.

Best Loved Folktales of the World, by Joanna Cole, Doubleday, 1983.

Favorite Folktales from Around the World, Jane Yolen, Pantheon, 1986.

44

CHAPTER 7

For Library Projects

★ **How do you find a story for a library storytelling workshop?**
★ **What kind of stories are best?**
★ **How do you choose just one?**

When you walk into any library you know there are probably millions of stories you could use. How do you choose one to tell?

Remember the three magic tips for choosing a story that you read about in Chapter 3.

1. Something your audience will like
2. Something that will accomplish your purpose—why you are telling the story
3. A story you like

This time you may start with the third reason, a story *you* really like. What kind of stories do you want to read? Mysteries? Fantasy? Science fiction? Since you will have to read many stories to find one you want to tell, pick the kinds you prefer to read.

Perhaps you would like to read stories about your hobbies. Do you have any collections? Are you involved in any sports? Is there something that you would like to know more about? Is there something you would like to share with the other kids?

The second rule may not help this time. You may not know who the audience will be and therefore cannot use them as a guide.

Instead of the audience, you could look at the other kids in your workshop for guidelines to help. What do you know about the other kids in the workshop? You may know a few of them personally. You may not know any of them. But all of you are looking for a story to tell, and for many of you it may be your first storytelling experience.

When Robbie went to the library that first day of summer vacation, he was looking for a nonfiction book that would help him identify new rocks in his collection. Rock collecting was his favorite hobby.

He liked stories about rock collecting, too. So when he saw the bulletin board poster about a new storytelling workshop, he signed up.

The theme of the workshop was American legends. Most of his friends were talking about stories of Paul Bunyan, Davy Crocket, and Johnny Appleseed. Those were fun stories, but everyone knew them. Robbie wanted a legend that his friends might not already know.

He walked slowly down the library aisle reading the titles off the spines of the books. He took a few books off the shelves. They were collections of legends. He ran his finger down the table of contents. Imagine his surprise when he found a legend about a talking rock and another about a storytelling stone.

He sat down on the floor in front of the book shelf and began reading. He soon discovered that both stories were based on the same old Seneca Indian legend. The original legend was about where stories came from, about how a storytelling rock first told them to a young boy. It was a perfect story for Robbie!

Robbie carefully read both versions again and discovered that they were quite different. The first version told about a young Seneca boy who was hunting for food for his family. When he stopped to rest by a stream in the forest, the Spirit of the Rock spoke to him and bargained with him. The Rock promised to tell him stories if he would give some of his hunt in exchange. He did, and the Rock told him many stories. The next day the boy came back and traded for more stories. He came back again and again, day after day, sometimes bringing friends to hear the talking rock that told stories. Then one day the stories stopped.

As many legends do, this one went on and on and seemed to combine several stories into one legend. It began with how the Spirit got into the Rock, how the boy got a bag to carry story reminders in, and how the boy later left the town and came back as an adult.

Robbie wasn't sure where the story really began and where it ended. The librarian suggested that he read as many versions of the legend as he could find, take the parts he liked best, and create his own version.

The second version of the story told about an orphan boy who was hunting food for his grandmother. When he sat on a stone to make more arrows, the stone spoke to him. He traded some of the birds he had caught for stories. The next day he brought the townspeople to hear the stone. It continued to tell stories for years. When it stopped, the stone told the boy that stories are a gift and to always request a gift in exchange for each story. Then, when he was too old to hunt, he would be able to trade stories for food.

Robbie liked some parts of both versions. He made a list of the parts that were the same:

1. The story was about a young boy.
2. A large stone (rock) talks to him.
3. The stone bargains for some of his hunt in exchange for the stories.
4. The stone tells stories to other people, too.
5. The stone stops telling stories

Then Robbie listed the extra parts he liked:

1. The boy hunted food for his grandmother.
2. The stone told him to take reminders.
3. The stone told him to always demand payment.

Robbie knew that a good modern story needed a beginning, a middle, and an ending. But he also knew that the other kids in the workshop watched TV, movies, and videos. He would have to make his story more exciting to interest them. So Robbie began asking himself questions to get more ideas.

1. If the young boy was hunting food for his grandmother, how did the other hunters feel? Did they laugh at his small bow and arrows?
2. If he traded some of his hunt for stories, would his grandmother run out of food before winter ended?
3. Could he use his stories to trade for food? How?

This is the story that Robbie told.

48

The Storytelling Stone

Long, long ago an orphan Indian boy was getting ready to go hunting. He pulled his small bow onto his shoulder and picked up a quiver of arrows.

"Ho! Hah!" laughed one of the hunters. "A boy is doing a man's work!" He laughed again. "Do you really think you can bring enough food home for your grandmother?"

The boy did not answer, but hurried into the forest. He was a good hunter and could get birds and rabbits even if he couldn't bring home the big deer that the men hunters did.

He worked hard all morning and had six fat birds by noon. He sat down on a large rock to fix his arrows.

"Do you want to hear a story?" asked a voice.

The boy looked but saw nobody. He went on fixing his arrows.

"I can tell you a story," the voice said again.

The boy stood up and looked at the stone. "Are you speaking to me?"

"If you give me one of your birds, I will tell you a story."

So the boy took one of the smaller birds and put it on the stone and he learned how the Sky Woman came to Earth.

When the story was over, the stone asked if he would like to hear another. He gave the stone another bird and learned how chipmunks got their stripes. Then he traded a third bird for a third story.

"Now," said the stone, "you must go home. But first take a black rock to remember the first story, a white stone to remember the second, and a yellow one to remember the third."

49

The boy picked up the stones and went home.

"Ho! Hah!" laughed all the hunters. "Three birds will not feed your grandmother this winter."

But his grandmother took the birds and said that she would dry the meat and use the feathers in a quilt.

The next day the boy went back into the forest to hunt. He got six rabbits before he came to the stone. Once again he traded rabbits for stories until he had only three left. Then the stone told him to take twigs from different trees to help him remember the new stories.

Once again the men laughed at him when he came home with only three rabbits. But his grandmother said she would dry the meat and use the fur for winter clothing.

On the third day, two of his friends offered to go with him to help him hunt. They got six birds and six rabbits by noon when they paused at the stone to eat some berries.

But the stone wanted a gift from *each* boy in return for its gift of story. So after three stories, the boys had only two birds and one rabbit left. Grandmother took what they gave her and was happy.

Every day for the next two weeks, the three boys hunted and traded for stories. Then, one afternoon, when a snowflakes began to fall, the stone told them that storytime was over. The stone reminded them to always demand a story or a gift in return for their stories and to always take a tiny memento to help remember new ones.

Winter came early that year and it was soon clear that the small amount of food the boys brought home would not last until spring.

"Let's have a storytelling feast," said the orphan boy. "Everyone can bring food to trade for stories." They had a gigantic feast and the boy told how Sky Woman Came To Earth.

Everyone liked the story and wanted to hear more. So they had another feast the next day and the boy told about how chipmunks got their stripes.

Everyday the boy traded stories for food or warm clothing, and his grandmother was never hungry or cold all that long winter.

"So this is my story," said Robbie. "And everyone who hears it owes me one in return." Robbie opened a small sack. "Here are tiny black stones to help you remember the story of the Storytelling Stone and where stories come from." He gave one little memento to each of the boys and girls in the audience to help them begin their own story collections.

For Further Reading

Legends, fairy tales, folk tales, and tall tales are all very good sources of stories for storytelling workshops.

Legends are stories that may have had some truth originally, but have been exaggerated. Tall tales are also stories that have been exaggerated but they are make believe and have never had any truth in them.

Fairy tales are stories about magic or supernatural worlds. They often include elves, genies, imps, sprites, gnomes, brownies, trolls, or leprechauns, as well as fairies.

Folk tales are often ethnic stories that have been handed down from generation to generation.

Here are some legends and fairy, folk, and tall tales you might want to adapt for a storytelling workshop.

A Children's Treasury of Folk and Fairy Tales, by Eric Protter, Beaufort, 1982.

A Treasury of American Folklore, by B. A. Botkin, Bonanza, 1983.

English Tairy Tales, by Joseph Jacobs, Dover, 1967.

Fairy Tales of Eastern Europe, by Neil Philip, Clarion Books, 1991.

Iroquois Stories, by Joseph Bruchac, The Crossing Press, 1985.

Johnny Appleseed: A Tall Tale, by Steven Kellogg, Morrow, 1988.

Realms of Gold: Myth and Legends From Around the World, by Ann Pilling, CKG Publishers, 1993.

Teeny-Tiny Folktales, by Jean Warren, Warren Publishing House, 1987.

The Tales of Uncle Remus--The Adventures of Brer Rabbit, by Julius Lester, Dial, 1987.

Whopper: Tall Tales and Other Lies Collected from American Folklore, by Alvin Schwartz, Lippincott, 1975.

Picture books have the easiest versions of the legends.

If you cannot find the books listed above, use the ones that are in your library. Look for legends in the nonfiction section of your library where books may have the Dewey Decimal number 398.

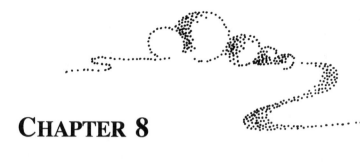

CHAPTER 8

At Religious Programs

★ **Do you have a favorite religious story?**
★ **Can you create a story to explain a custom?**
★ **How can stories help you do the right things?**

Most religious stories started long ago as storytelling stories. They were passed from generation to generation by fathers telling their sons, mothers telling their daughters, and church leaders telling their followers.

Retelling The Old Stories

When spoken stories were passed from older people to younger ones, the storyteller was expected to keep the story in the true or original form. He couldn't change it or adapt it. He simply had to remember it and retell it.

Today most of the old stories have been written down. Some

have been rewritten as easy versions or picture books for very young children to read and understand.

It is these easy versions that you want to use if you are planning to do a retelling. Although you can read and use material from other versions, if you want, use the simple story as your basic outline.

You will find opportunities for retellings during your religious holidays. Religious leaders are encouraging children to tell stories as a way to learn and understand the history of their faith.

Holiday retellings are a good chance to use costumes or props to re-create a long ago setting. You might be able to add a musical instrument or background music. Some stories have puppet figures that you can buy to help tell the story.

Explaining Meanings

Sometimes you can modify a story to explain its meaning. Take the story of Noah's Ark, for example. It has been used for many different reasons. You could point out that it wasn't raining when God first asked Noah to build an ark. You could stress that Noah did what his god asked him to do even though it wasn't what everyone else was doing. You might concentrate on the animals and Noah's concern for saving them. Or you could focus on the rainbow. There are rainbow stories in almost every culture. How are they alike? How are they different?

Sometimes you can create a new story to explain the meaning of some traditional customs. Why do you do certain things in your religious community? How would you explain them to others of a different faith? Can you make your explanation into a story?

54

Creating Here And Now Stories

You can also take the theme or meaning from old stories and translate them into modern ones. This is how many stories are created for religious magazines. Take a simple theme, such as why you should tell the truth, why help a friend, or why you should never cheat. Can you create a story to explain those ideas?

Read your religious literature for ideas. How can you change the characters to make them more like boys and girls in your class? How can you change the setting? A story about cheating in a soccer game can also be about cheating in a volleyball game.

By changing characters or setting, you can adapt religious stories to be appropriate for any audience.

For Further Reading

You might want to read short stories in some of the following children's magazines for contemorary ideas that you can use for storytelling in your own religious community.

Clubhouse, Your Story Hour
Box 15
Berrien Springs MI 49103

Crusader
Box 7259
Grand Rapids MI 49510

Faith 'n Stuff
Guideposts Assoc. Inc.
Carmel, New York 10512-1999

My Friend, A Magazine for Children
50 St. Paul's Ave.
Boston MA 02130

Pockets, Devotional Magazine for Children
The Upper Room
Box 189
Nashville TN 37202

The Friend
50 E. North Temple
Sault Lake City, UT 84150

Shofar
43 Northcote Dr.
Melville NY 11747

Touch
Calvinettes
Box 7259
Grand Rapids, MI 49510

Venture
Christian Service Brigade
Box 150
Wheaton, IL 60189

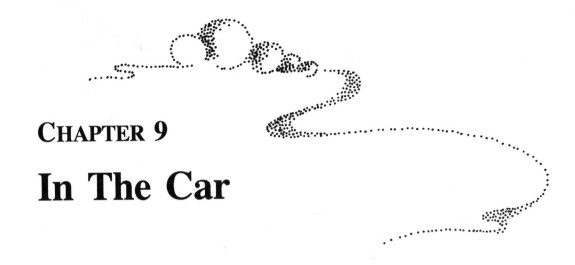

CHAPTER 9

In The Car

★ **Do you ride in the car while your relatives run errands?**
★ **Do you ride in car pools to classes or activities?**
★ **Does your family drive on vacation?**

You can use the time you spend riding in a car to play storytelling games, create mini-stories, and act out finger puppet plays. It makes car rides a lot more fun.

Storytelling Games

There are many storytelling games that will help you become a better storyteller. You can play voice games to help you learn how to change your voice when you pretend to be another character. You can play memory games to help you remember stories and story patterns. You can also play singing games, adding games, and alliteration games.

Voice Games

One kind of voice game is to change the meaning of a sentence by how you say it. You probably have asked your parents this question many times.

> How *long* before we get there?
> How long before *we* get there?
> How long before we get *there*?

Which word did you stress? Does stressing a different word change the meaning of the sentence? How many ways can you say this sentence?

Try stressing different words in the following sentences.

> I just saw the teeny tiniest bug.
> How long has your uncle been in France?
> Did you really let her borrow your sweater?

Next time you are riding in a car, try making up some of your own sentences, and then see how many different ways you can say them.

Another kind of voice game to play is to pretend you are another person. You can ask or answer a question as this other person. Take the sentences above that you used to practice changing the meaning and pretend you are a football player, a policeman, a kindergartener, a mother, a waitress at a restaurant, or a make-believe creature with a *very* different voice.

Remembering Games

You have probably played remembering games at parties. There are many of them and many kinds. One example is the Going On A Trip game. You can start the game by saying, "I am going on a trip and taking one pair of jeans." Another person in the car could say, "I am going on a trip and taking one pair of jeans and two red sweaters." A third person could add, "I am going on a trip and taking one pair of jeans, two red sweaters, and three pairs of shoes." Every person in the car should have a turn. Each person must repeat the whole list and add one more item. When one person makes a mistake, you can start over with a new sentence. There is no winning or losing. It's just fun and you get better and can remember longer lists each time you play.

Another kind of a memory game is the Add An Adjective game. You can start the game by making up a sentence such as, "I had a dog." The next person adds a descriptive word to the sentence, and could say, "I had a big dog." Each person in the car must add a descriptive word. It could go on like this.

I had a dog.
I had a big dog.
I had a big black dog.
I had a big black shaggy dog.
I had a lazy big black shaggy dog.
I had a lazy hungry big black shaggy dog.

When you can't think of any more words, start a new sentence. Sometimes the sentences get really funny so keep them going as long as you can. The longer you can keep a sentence going, the funnier it will be.

You can do the same thing with alliteration. That means each word you add must begin with the same letter.

> Look at the mountains.
> Look at the many mountains.
> Look at the many majestic mountains.
> Look at the many more majestic mountains.

Singing Games

There are many singing games that are like memory games. Have you ever sung Old MacDonald Had A Farm?

Singing games are good for car pool rides or field trips. Some good ones are And The Green Grass Grew All Around, Found A Peanut, and 99 Bottles Of Pop. If you don't know them, just suggest singing one of them the next time you are on a school bus. Someone will know it and will get everyone started. Your friends will then suggest others. See how many new singing games you can learn and collect.

Mini-Stories

Mini-stories are also games. They are created from the things you see as you are riding in a car. They can start with a person, a place, or something that is happening. You create the story by asking the who, what, why, when, where and how questions. For example, if you see an old lady crossing the street, you might ask:

60

Who could that person be?
Where is that person going?
What is that person going to do when she arrives?
Why is that person going there?
When will that person arrive?
How will that person get there?

Look out the car window. The story must start with something you see. You can create as many stories as you want. Everyone in the car can help with the stories.

You can also make up mini-stories by asking *what-if* or *I wonder why*. But, once again, the story must start with something you see. For example, you may be stopped for a red light. You might ask *what if* it never turned green. What would happen then? *What if* the road you are traveling on just ended? What would you do? See how many *what if* stories you can make up.

Finger Puppet Plays

Traveling in a car is a great time to play with finger puppets. Everyone in the car is close enough to see your fingers move as you tell the story.

You will need to make the finger puppets before your car ride, but you can have a collection of finger puppets that you take with you on every trip. You can use traditional stories or you can make up new stories for the puppets.

The best stories for finger puppet plays have five or ten characters. Two traditional stories are The Little Red Hen and The Gingerbread Boy.

In The Little Red Hen, use your thumb for the hen and the other fingers can be any animals you want. For example, if you have finger puppets for a rabbit, duck, monkey, and chipmunk, use them. Remember to use a different voice for each animal.

The Little Red Hen
Finger Puppet Play

LITTLE RED HEN: Look, I have found some wheat.
                Who will help me plant this wheat?
CAT: Not I.
DOG: Not I.
PIG: Not I.
COW: Not I.
LITTLE RED HEN: Then I'll plant it *all by myself.*
YOU: And she did.

LITTLE RED HEN: Who will help me water the wheat?
CAT: Not I.
DOG: Not I.
PIG: Not I.
COW: Not I.
LITTLE RED HEN: Then I'll water it *all by myself.*
YOU: And she did.
      When the wheat began to grow, she asked for help again.

LITTLE RED HEN: Who will help me weed the wheat?

CAT: Not I.
DOG: Not I.
PIG: Not I.
COW: Not I.
LITTLE RED HEN: Then I'll weed it *all by myself.*
You: And she did.
        The wheat ripened. And the hen asked for help again.

LITTLE RED HEN: Who will help me harvest the wheat?
CAT: Not I.
DOG: Not I.
PIG: Not I.
COW: Not I.
LITTLE RED HEN: Then I'll harvest it *all by myself.*
YOU: And she did.

LITTLE RED HEN: Who will help me take this wheat to the mill
                to be ground into flour?
CAT: Not I.
DOG: Not I.
PIG: Not I.
COW: Not I.
LITTLE RED HEN: Then I'll take it to the mill *all by myself.*
YOU: And she did.

LITTLE RED HEN: Who will help me make cookies?
CAT: Not I.
DOG: Not I.

PIG: Not I.
COW: Not I.
LITTLE RED HEN: Then I'll make cookies *all by myself.*
YOU: And she did.
   And the cookies smelled so good.

LITTLE RED HEN: Now, who will help me eat the cookies?
CAT: I will.
DOG: I will.
PIG: I will.
COW: I will.
LITTLE RED HEN: OH NO!
   I planted the wheat *all by myself.*
   I watered it *all by myself.*
   I weeded it *all by myself.*
   I harvested it *all by myself.*
   I took it to the mill *all by myself.*
   I baked the cookies *all by myself.*
   And now I'm going to eat them
      all by myself.
YOU: And she did, right down to the very last crumb.

Other stories you can use:
   Chicken Little
   Bremen Town Musicians
   Snow White And the Seven Dwarfs

CHAPTER 10

Family Storytelling Time

★ **What kind of stories do families share?**
★ **How do you discover good family stories?**
★ **What are together time stories?**

A good way to uncover some interesting family stories is to start telling a story yourself. To get a story you must give one away.

Family Stories

Your story doesn't have to be long. It can be as simple as something that happened to you at school. Jason started a family storytelling time once with just one simple sentence. "I was just trying to help," he said, "and everything went wrong."

How everything can go wrong is a story pattern. You do something which someone misunderstands and they do something in response which is also misunderstood and it continues on and on.

65

Jason's father said it was a lot like trying to fix the plumbing in their old house. When he tried to fix one leak, something else broke. This caused something else to get bent, which caused another problem. He had to end up getting a whole new sink and cabinet.

Jason's sister told about how everything went wrong because she got to a meeting five minutes late. She didn't get to talk to someone before the meeting who had some new information. Everything went downhill from there.

Jason's mother told how everything went wrong because of a telephone call. His brother told about how the same thing happened to him when he forgot one piece for his science project. When Jason's friend stopped by, he jumped into the storytelling with another story.

Family storytelling time can be sharing jokes, embarrassing moments, fun things, and how sometimes everything works out okay.

Secrets Of The Past

Family history stories are a little harder to collect. They may start with a single sentence, or part of a conversation. They may start with a comment about an old photograph, trophy, or keepsake. Then, you might have to do some detective work and interviewing to get the whole story or to create a story from the information you gather.

Interviewing family members, especially grandparents, aunts, and uncles can produce some good information. Don't walk into the room with a notepad and pencil, however, if you expect anyone to tell you ancient secrets. A casual comment can usually start the stories.

Mandy asked her mother the first question while they were driving to her gymnastic lessons. She just happened to ask if her mother had ever taken gymnastics when she was a girl.

Her mother chuckled. "No, there were no gymnastic lessons in our city, but my mother, your grandmother, drove through rush hour traffic twice a week to take me to horseback riding lessons.

"Like Aunt Lisa?" Mandy asked. "She has so many trophies and ribbons."

Her mother chuckled again. "I won a horse trophy before your Aunt Lisa ever learned to ride, even before she was bitten by the first horse she ever met."

Mandy knew there was a good horse story there, but they had arrived at the gymnasium. She didn't forget. The next day Mandy asked her grandmother about the riding lessons, and if her aunt really had been bitten by a horse.

Grandmother didn't chuckle. She laughed loudly. "Oh my, do I remember, Mandy. The snow was a foot deep, but your mother and Lisa insisted on driving to the stables. Of course there were no lessons that day, but the girls had brought carrots for their favorite horses. Your mother's horse was polite, but Patches loved carrots so much he took a gigantic bite of Aunt Lisa's carrot and her hand. He wouldn't let go." Grandma laughed again. "Your aunt learned how to feed carrots to horses that day. Ask her about it sometime."

Mandy made a mental note to see her aunt for more details, but she had a funny feeling that Aunt Lisa, a professional rider, might not want that story told outside the family. Instead, she asked her grandmother about the trophy her mother had won.

When they went to look for it, Mandy and her grandmother could only find a box of Aunt Lisa's trophies, ones she had won when she was Mandy's age. Grandmother wouldn't let Mandy touch them, because they belonged to Aunt Lisa.

On Thanksgiving Day, when the family gathered at Grandmother's house, Mandy asked her aunt about the trophies. They sat down together and unpacked the box. Aunt Lisa had a special story about all but one, which Mandy's mother claimed as her long lost prize.

As Mandy suspected, Aunt Lisa did *not* want the hand biting story told. She did suggest that Mandy come to her stables, take a few lessons, and begin to create her own horse stories.

Now Mandy's mother picks her up after school and drives her across town during rush hour traffic to riding lessons at Aunt Lisa's stables.

Mandy has a collection of horse tales which she shares with friends, classmates, and family. And she has a new hobby.

Conversations are seldom complete full stories. You will need to create stories from the information you collect.

Together Time Stories

More and more families today are doing activities and taking vacations together. They are jogging, bike riding, camping, horseback riding, fishing, and boating. They are taking mini-trips to zoos, museums, and parks. And, they are taking long vacations at resorts across the country.

Since families are playing together, they are also sharing tales together. At the end of the day or the end of the trip, families are sharing stories about what happened to them. Sometimes these story times are impromptu and everyone joins in to add more details or contribute "missing parts."

Some families, however, are really polishing up their act. The

68

Smith family, for example, took a mini-camping vacation over a four-day holiday weekend. Mrs Smith loves to draw and brought a sketch book along with her. Mr. Smith has a hobby of recording sounds and took a tape recorder. Fifteen-year-old Brad rented a camcorder. Twelve-year-old Cora loves crafts and collected shells and rocks. Eight-year-old Mark loves bugs, beetles, worms, and furry critters. Five-year old Angela collected postcards from every place they stopped.

Everyone in this family found something special on their trip and they created a family story. Now they present their 30-minute presentation for luncheon or dinner programs. They have also given their show at the local library.

Whether your family is only your father and you; your grand-other and you; or your mom, step-dad, and six brothers and sisters, sharing stories, current or past, can be a lot of fun.

For Further Reading

For ideas on the kind of stories you can tell about your family, you might want to read the following books.

The Stories Julian Tells, by Ann Cameron, Random House, 1981.
Our Mountain, by Ellen Harvey Showell, Bradbury Press, 1991.
A Celebration of American Family Folklore, Tales and Traditions from the Smithsonian Collection, by Steven J. Zeitlin, Amy J. Kotkin, and Holly Cutting Baker, Pantheon Books, 1982.

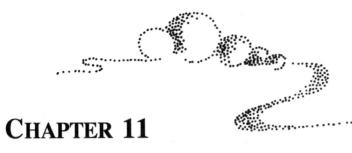

CHAPTER 11

For Babysitter Storytime

★ **How can stories help you take care of younger kids?**
★ **How can stories make kids behave?**
★ **How can stories make you the babysitter kids ask for?**

Many babysitters read to children, but more and more sitters are discovering that stories do more than entertain kids. They can help with behavior problems. And, make them popular babysitters!

Creative Toy Stories

Whether a child is six months or six years, you can pick up one of their toys and create a story. It may be just a simple tale about a little lamb that goes for a walk around the crib. Or it may be about a teddy bear that does exercises.

The most successful stories are the ones the children help tell. Get them started by asking questions. Why is a doll or stuffed animal looking tired, or sad, or hungry today? Where is the little train going today and why? Who is coming to visit the dollhouse people?

Encourage the children to tell most of the story by continuing to ask questions whenever they seem to pause. See how long you can keep it going.

With older kids, you can enlist the aid of aliens from another planet. What would they think of the game you are playing or what would they do with a coloring book?

You might create a series of stories, a continuing saga, with one particular toy each time you sit. With a set of blocks you could build a different house for mini-monsters each time you came. A train set, puppet stage, or craft can be the basis for stories only you can create when you babysit with them.

Toys That Encourage Stories

Construction blocks
Dollhouses
Farm sets
Castle sets
Puppets
Tents
Train sets
Cars and trucks
Crayons and paper
Doctor sets

Helper Stories

Helper stories are the ones you can use, or make up, to get kids to do what they should but don't always want to do.

If it's time for lunch and they don't want to stop playing, you can tell about a puppy who didn't want to eat his meal. If it's bedtime, you could create a story about a hippopotamus that is looking for the best place to sleep.

If the children are afraid of a strong wind, make up a story about what causes wind and why it cannot hurt them. If they get a scratch, try a spin-off of the tooth fairy and create a bandage fairy that rewards brave children with good luck fairy dust.

If something is lost, tell how invisible gnomes and brownies like to hide things from children and how kids can learn to find the secret hiding places.

Try using stories to change behavior that is hard for you to manage. Make up a story about the behavior problem.

Rita used stories to help her get through her most difficult babysitting job. She had taken care of the three Johnson children for almost a year. Recently, Mr. Johnson had remarried, and there were now five children.

It was not taking care of five children that worried Rita. What concerned her was that she didn't know the new children or whether they got along together.

Whenever she babysat for the Johnsons, she made up stories with the children. Each child had a stuffed animal that became a character in the story. It was a continuing series of stories that always used the same characters.

Rita searched through her old toys and found a not-too-worn-out rabbit and a lamb. She took them with her the first time she took care of all five.

She told the children that two new animals were coming to live with them. She asked the three Johnson children to show their new brother and sister how they made up stories with the old toys. Then she added the two new ones and asked everyone to join in.

She soon discovered that the children really liked each other, but that there were a few jealousies. She now knew what to watch out for and some conflicts to try to avoid.

PART III
How To Tell a Good Story

CHAPTER 12

Making The Story Yours

★ **What if someone else tells the story you want to tell?**
★ **How can you make your story different?**
★ **How can you make each telling a special event?**

No two people tell the same story the same way, and no one person tells the same story the same way twice. Each storyteller has his own style. A storyteller makes each telling a unique experience.

How do you make a story your very own? How can you make every one of your tellings a special occasion?

When you begin to study a story, you will have many opportunities to adapt it and make it your own. Read your story through five times, each time looking for something special.

1. Read For Fun
The first time, read the story for fun to capture the entire

story. If there is some obvious change, make a note of it, but don't worry about changes yet.

2. Study The Characters

During the second reading, study the characters. What kind of person is the main character. Does he or she have a special voice, any unusual characteristics, needs or wants. What about the other characters. Will you use another voice to portray them? Make notes in a notebook about the ideas you have. You may not use them all or any of them, but noting your early impressions of the characters will help you learn the story and tell it better.

3. Study Story Structure

The third time you read the story, look for story structure, sequence, and plot elements. What happens? In what order? Is there a pattern of events? Do you want to change this order by adding or skipping something?

4. Look For Special Catchwords and Phrases

Read the story again for catchwords or special phrases. If there aren't any, create some to give the story more interest, to make your audience anticipate the next part or participate in a chorus.

5. Imagine The Setting

Read the story the fifth time to pick up the scene or setting. Is there anything special about the location where the story takes place? You can add details or create a scene if the original story doesn't give enough description. Don't add too many.

78

At this time you might want to consider if you need any story helpers? Do you want to use a costume or prop, such as a ball or bat. Do you want to sing a phrase or have any background music? Do you want to use a puppet? Will you need any signs or posters. Look at Chapter 16 for other ideas for story helpers.

CHAPTER 13

Learning The Story

★ **How do storytellers learn their stories?**
★ **What is a story map?**
★ **How can props help you remember a story?**

Some people can read a story once or twice and remember it well enough to tell it. Most people have to work a little harder.

First, remember that you *learn* a story, you don't memorize it. You may memorize an opening or closing sentence or a catch phrase or two, but never the whole story.

After you have studied and adapted the story, you are ready to make what storytellers call a story map to help you remember the sequence of events in the story. You can use either words or pictures to make this map.

Divide your story map into a beginning, middle and ending. It should look something like this.

Beginning	Middle	Ending

Now list the things that happen in the beginning. The beginning should introduce the main character and what his problem is.

The middle of the story should include what the character does and what happens to him.

The ending should include how the character solves his problem and how the story ends.

For an example let's use "The Magic Dream Doll" story from Chapter 5.

Beginning	Middle	Ending
Maria's Grandmother shows how to make a Dream Doll Grandmother tells how Dream Doll is magic Maria does not believe	Maria carries doll in her pocket. Takes doll out when lonely but cannot talk to doll. Nobody remembers her birthday.	Maria cries to the Dream Doll She tells it her dreams Her dreams come true on her birthday Keep a Dream Doll in your pocket

Sometimes a story may not have an obvious beginning, middle, and ending. It may depend more on an order of events. The story of "The Little Red Hen" in Chapter 9 is a good example of this kind of story.

A picture poster map, like the one on page 84, could help you remember this kind of story. Each picture represents something the Little Red Hen asked.

Who will help me *plant* the wheat? (shovel and fork)
Who will help me *water* the wheat? (watering can)
Who will help me *weed* the wheat? (hoe and rake)
Who will help me *harvest* the wheat? (plant)
Who will help me *take the wheat to the mill*? (mill)
Who will help me *make cookies*? (bowl and cookies)
Who will help me *eat the cookies*? (table and chairs)

Although you may want to create picture poster maps on your computer like this example, you can also sketch simple drawings that you make yourself.

You could create your map as a horizontal or vertical banner instead of a poster. Hang it on your bedroom wall until you have learned the story. You will be able to picture these maps in your mind when you tell the story.

You can also use memory helpers or props to remember the order of events in your story. These props can be items that you place on a table and pick up as your story goes along.

Go back to Chapter 4 and read the story of "The Trails Signs" again to see how Cindy used the stones as props in her story.

The Little Red Hen

CHAPTER 14

Practicing Telling Your Story

★ **How do you practice telling a story?**
★ **Can mirrors and tapes help?**
★ **Can friends and family help?**

Every storyteller practices in his or her own way. Some methods work for one person and not for another. Experiment with some of the ideas in this chapter to see what works best for you.

Every storyteller must watch certain things during practice. One storyteller may naturally talk too fast and will need practice time to learn to speak slowly and clearly. Another storyteller may not talk loud enough. You will soon discover what things you need to watch.

In Front Of Stuffed Toys or Pets

If you have a collection of stuffed animals, you may want to line them up on a table or bed to be your first audience. This audience is usually very patient and understanding of your first attempts. And they are never too critical!

Pet animals sometimes listen, too. Alex practiced his story by talking to cows in his father's feed lot. Andrea's family has a big fat cat named Maximillian who listens to her stories.

Greg had trouble getting enough expression in his voice until he began telling stories to his dog. Because the dog could not under-stand what he was saying, it only responded to how sad or happy, slow or fast, or loud or soft his voice was. Greg learned to change his voice often to keep the dog interested.

Before Family Members

Many boys and girls practice stories by telling them to their parents, aunts, and uncles. Grandparents sometimes have more time and therefore are often are more patient. Family members can help you with speed and pacing. Are you talking too fast or too slow for them to under-stand you? Are you putting in extra words like "umm" or "uh" or repeating words? Do you need to pause for your audience to laugh or respond?

With Friends

Encourage your friends, not to just listen to your stories, but to help you become a better storyteller. Friends are great for helping you keep a story exciting. Tell them what you want them to look for. Watch how they listen. Are they interested? Are they excited. Are they falling asleep? Do they look around the room or work on another project while you are talking?

Maybe they could suggest some hand or body movements that

you could use. Maybe they could think of some props or costumes that might add interest. Get them interested in being part of your production.

In Front Of Mirrors

Some storytellers like to practice in front of mirrors. Others find it distracting to watch themselves while they are talking. They say it is like trying to pat your head and rub your stomach at the same time.

Try using a mirror to watch your hand gestures, body movement, and facial expressions. See if it works for you.

On Audio or Video Tape (Camcorder)

If you have a camcorder you can use or rent, make a video of your performance. Don't try to perform for the camera, however, because it doesn't respond. Tell your story to a live audience of family or friends and have someone record your performance. Play the tape back several times and look for different things each time. How can you improve it?

An audio tape recorder can also be very helpful. Although you cannot see yourself, you can hear what your audience hears. Can you improve the expression in your voice, speed of delivery, volume, or pauses?

At Storytelling Clubs And Workshops

Practicing in front of a group of kids who also tell stories is one of the best places to get expert help. This audience knows what to look for and can make some very good suggestions. Remember to keep comments positive, so you can use the ideas to improve your telling.

Clubs and workshops are also good places to learn how loud you need to talk. How can you talk softly and be loud enough to be heard in the back of the room?

CHAPTER 15

Telling The Story

★ **How do you begin?**
★ **What if you are scared?**
★ **What if you forget something?**

Just as choosing the right story depends on when and where you plan to tell it, *how* you tell your story also depends on your audience.

A story you tell to friends around a campfire will be different from the one you tell the child you are babysitting. And both will be different from the one you tell in an auditorium on parents night.

It could be the same story, adapted three different ways. But *how* you tell it will be different, also. You need to adapt your story and your method of telling it for each audience.

Getting Your Audience Ready

Whether you are telling your story to an audience of one or one hundred, you will have more success if your audience is ready to listen.

When Marla was getting ready to tell her finger puppet story at a slumber party, the other kids were still giggling about the jokes they had been sharing. Marla slipped her hand into her finger puppet glove, but held one finger down.

"I'm sorry," she told her friends. "I can't start yet. One of my finger puppets is still giggling."

She waited. Then, with her other hand, she lifted the finger and asked if it was ready to help tell the story.

"Hee, hee!" giggled the finger. Marla continued to wait.

When everyone else was waiting, too, Marla began.

When Luann takes her foldout castle to her babysitting jobs, she always saves it for quiet time. She lets the small children play active games to wear off some energy first. Then when it is rest time or almost bedtime, she slowly begins unfolding the castle. She asks the children to help her and they begin to talk about the characters, what kind of day it is at the castle, or what might happen in the story today. At this point, she has the children ready to listen to a story.

At Randy's storytelling club, one of the boys or girls lights a candle to bring storytelling magic into the room.

One storyteller likes to take small audiences on a tour through a house or building looking for the storytelling room. She then leads them to a place that has been prepared for storytelling with low light and cushions to sit on.

If a real trip is not possible, you might have your audience take a pretend trip with you to an imaginary storytelling place.

Some storytellers, when speaking to a large audience, just

introduce themselves and their story because the audience is already prepared to listen. When you speak to a large group, you might just give your name and the title of the story as Jolinda did.

> "I'm Jolinda Lee Allen and I'm
> going to tell you the story of
> Chicken Little."

Sometimes, you may want to tell something about your story to draw the audience into it, like Pete did.

> "I'm Pete Potter and I'm going
> to tell you one of the tall tales
> about what happened to Paul
> Bunyan and his ox, Babe, one
> very, very cold winter day."

After an introduction like Jolinda or Pete used, you may want to pause for a few moments until your audience is listening. Count to ten or think about your character to get into the mood yourself.

If there is a catch phrase that the audience will repeat to help you tell the story, you can rehearse it with the audience before you start. This helps get a large audience ready to listen. Let's say you are telling a story of farm animals and at the end of each part you say, "Old MacDonald Had A Farm" and your audience says "E-I-E-I-O." Practice saying the phrase and let the audience chant the response so they know how and when to say it. Then begin your story.

Handling Problems

Every storyteller has some problem that he has to watch for or something that happens in one story that he has to overcome.

Some kids are a little nervous when they first stand up in front of a classroom or an auditorium full of parents.

Even though Kevin's teacher tried to help by explaining that the audience was looking at his story not him, he was still nervous. Then he saw people in the audience who had heard the story while he was practicing. He pretended he was still practicing and tried to remember what they had told him. He told the story the best he ever had.

Greta, however, was terrified when she first stood in front of her class. She remembered her storyteller aunt's advice about giving your fear to your characters. Fortunately Greta's story was a ghost story with a scary part near the beginning. Greta overdid it. She made her main character terrified and trembling. When she looked up and around her audience to make eye contact, everyone was glued to her every word. It was then that Greta first felt that magic storytelling feeling, the thrill of holding an audience captive. She dragged out the second scary part and skipped through the transition to the third scary part. The third part was really the hardest for her. By this time she was having so much fun it was hard to make her main character frightened anymore.

Eric had a problem in the middle of his Irish tale about the tricks of the wee folk. It seemed his audience was going to sleep. Since his tale was about the tricks elves and gnomes play on people, he continued to lull them on with sort of a droning voice. Then, suddenly, POP! Out from behind a bush jumped a leprechaun who snatched the prize and ran away. And that was the end. The audience

92

woke up to realize that they, too, had been tricked.

Michael had trouble with numbers. He knew that it didn't really matter in his story if he used five, fifteen, and fifty or one, ten and twenty. It just needed to be a growing number. But it needed to be a *reasonable* growing number.

When Michael started to tell his story at the festival, he was so nervous that he forgot the numbers he had planned to use. They just dropped out of his story as if someone had opened a trap door and they escaped, leaving all these holes in his story.

So he improvised. When he got to the first spot, he said hundreds. When he got to the second place, he said thousands, and when he got to the third spot, he looked up and saw his older brother with hands clapped to his ears shaking his head.

Michael stopped, shrugged, and said his hero really had trouble counting to a million but he was sure it was at least that many. Everyone laughed, and Michael finished his story.

Later, he learned that there were many storytellers in the audience that also had trouble with numbers.

It is these warm sharing moments and the thrill of holding an audience that help put the magic into storytelling and make it different than stories you watch in movies or on TV.

CHAPTER 16

Using Story Helpers

★ **Should you use a hat or a whole costume?**
★ **Can you sing or draw while telling your story?**
★ **Would puppets help you tell the tale?**

There are many story helpers that can make you less nervous or get you into the mood for your storytelling. Sometimes these helpers add just the right touch to make your story something special. You won't want to use all of them, but you might want to consider one or two.

Dressing Up In Costumes

Halloween is a good time to tell stories in costume. While you are dressed as the Wicked Witch or the Good Fairy, tell a story as if this character were telling it. There are a lot of good Halloween stories that you could use.

Other times of the year are good costume times, too. Dressed as Santa Claus, you could tell how Santa overslept one Christmas, got lost in a storm, or found Rudolph. You might make up a short story for a pilgrim, astronaut, pirate, fireman, or soldier. Or you could dress in an ethnic costume to tell a story from a particular culture.

Costume Parts

Sometimes you don't need a whole costume. A hat, cape, glove or jacket may do the trick.

Ethan used a cowboy hat and boots to tell his wild west tales about Sheriff Bill and the gunman.

Randy used a baseball mitt and ball to tell about the ninth inning surprise.

Carlotta wore bracelets, necklaces and ankle bells to weave her gypsy magic.

Masks and Face Paint

A mask can help you feel like the character in your story.

While you could wear an elaborate paper mache mask of a dinosaur or dragon, sometimes a simple one is just as effective. Jason made three paper plate masks which he used to tell the parts of three characters in his story.

All the children in one workshop experimented with face paint to portray characters for their stories. Some of them were clowns, some were animals, some were monsters. One girl did a traditional mime face and tried a brief story in pantomime.

Using Props

Sometimes props can add to your story and keep your audience interested. Sometimes they just make you feel more at ease. They can be story reminders to help you remember which part of a story sequence comes first, second or third.

Toni used nested Matrioska dolls to tell a story about a great grandmother, grandmother, mother, older sister, and baby. Netta used a set of nested eggs to tell an Easter story.

If your story is about football, a clock, or a teddy bear, you might be able to use these props as part of your story.

Adding Music or Sound Effects

If you play a musical instrument, you can use it to help tell your story. Some professional storytellers use a guitar and sing their stories (ballads). Some only use the instrument for a verse that is repeated again and again in the story.

One young girl used a flute in a story about a fairy flute player. A boy shook bells whenever his leprechaun appeared, because the magic creature wore bells on his shoes.

Many storytellers use drums or rattles to highlight parts of their stories. Some boys and girls make their own drums and rattles. Look for library books about musical instruments that you can make.

Some storytellers use background music to create a mood. You can get many sound-effect tapes. Marc used a tape of sea sounds for his surfing stories. Heidi created her own tape of eerie sounds for her ghostly tales.

Working With Puppets

Which comes first, the puppet or the story. It is a little like the chicken or the egg. With puppets, it can be either one. You may create a story for a puppet you have made or make a puppet to help tell a story.

There are so many kinds of puppets. You could use finger puppets, hand puppets, stick figures, shadow puppets or marionettes. Experiment with different kinds for different occasions.

Kari used a glove of finger puppets to tell stories at parties. One family carried a box of finger puppets in their car on long vacation trips. A grandmother made several sets of crocheted finger puppets that she carried in her purse when she babysat. They were just the right size for tiny fingers.

Drawing Your Way Through A Story

On a chalk board or large poster board you can draw as you tell your story. There are many stories that are designed for drawing and telling or you can create your own. Some drawings cleverly develop a unique character or scene for a special ending. Others just illustrate the tale.

Tammi's storytelling club had fun with sidewalk chalk and shadow pictures. At first they outlined each others' shadows on the sidewalk and then added details as they made up stories. Later they started posing to create monsters and silly stories.

Using Signs, Posters, Banners, And Flags

Some stories can use signs, posters, banners or flags. You can print these out with many computer programs to produce unique and fun additions to your story.

Signs can help in scene or time changes. Parading back and forth with a sign can also add humor.

Cutting And Folding

Many storytellers cut paper plates and newspapers while telling a story. The cutouts and cutups become props in their stories.

Brenda folds a newspaper in accordion pleats and cuts out dolls. She then unfolds a long chain of children holding hands for her friendship story. Sometimes she cuts out animals.

Look for books on cutting and folding stories. You can modify or adapt them to fit your story.

Creating Crafts

Just as some storytellers draw or cut as part of their story, some people like to create a craft as they tell a story. If there is some craft that you enjoy that can be demonstrated as part of a story, you might want to try it.

Crafts work well to get your friends into a storytelling mood at a party or club meeting. At Angela's birthday party, everyone made hand puppets out of lunch bags. While making them, each kid told about her puppet, what it liked or wanted, what it was afraid of, and where it wanted to go. When they were done, everyone told a tiny tale using the puppets. Later, the guests took the puppets home as favors.

In Julio's class, the children made pinatas and hung them around the room. Then the children found and shared pinata stories.

Looking For Ideas

You may find many craft books in the library with the Dewey Decimal number 745. You will also get ideas by walking through a

99

craft store or fabric shop. Look at the booklets and leaflets in these stores. Be sure to practice the craft you plan to demonstrate before you attempt to use it with a story.

Here are a few books to give you some ideas for story helpers.

Build a Doodle, by Beverly Armstrong, The Learning Works, 1985.

Costumes, by Clare Beaton, Warwick Press, 1990

Easy-To-Make Costumes, by Kathryn Harrison & Valerie Kohn, Sterling Publishing Company, 1992

Great Newspaper Crafts, by F. Virginia Walter, Sterling Publishing Company, 1991.

Hidden Stories in Plants, by Anne Pellowski, Macmillian Publishing Co. 1990.

I Can Draw Cars, Trucks, Trains and Other Wheels, by Tony Tallarico, Simon & Schuster, 1981

Make Costumes! For Creative Play, by Priscilla Hershberger, North Light Books, 1992.

McCalls Creates Finger Tales, Leaflet #14029, McCall Pattern Company. Shows how to make finger puppet gloves for Old MacDonald Had A Farm, Little Red Riding Hood, Three Billy Goats Gruff, Goldilocks & The Three Bears, The Three Little Pigs, Hansel And Gretel, Jack And The Beanstalk, and Five Little Monkeys.

CHAPTER 17

Mastering The Art

★ **Have you enjoyed telling a story?**
★ **Would you like to tell more stories?**
★ **Would you like to be a really good storyteller?**

Although you can read about where to tell stories, and where to find stories, and how to adapt them, you must listen to real live storytellers in order to master the art of storytelling.

Listen to Other Storytellers

Many adults make their living as storytellers, while some tell stories only as a hobby. Look for storytellers at local festivals, library programs, park programs, or in your school.

When you are sitting in the audience listening to a live storyteller you have a wonderful opportunity to study the performer and the audience together. What does the storyteller do to get the attention of the audience? What does he or she do to weave that magic spell?

What kind of body language does the storyteller use? Watch his or her arms, body, and head. Watch their eyes. Do the movements help tell the story or create an image?

How does the audience respond? Do they help tell the story? Are they quiet and glued to his every word? Do they jump in surprise at a sudden ending?

How do you feel? Are you so interested in the story that you forget to watch the storyteller?

How does the storyteller react to the audience?

Watch Videos of Storytellers

Because it is so easy to get caught up in a story during a live performance, you may not be able to watch everything a storyteller does. Watching the "reruns" on a video tape can give you a chance to study exactly what the teller does.

If you watch a storyteller tell the story again, he will do something different because each telling is a new event. Videos capture one telling so you can study it more closely. It is like professional football players reviewing game tapes to improve their play.

Listen To Audio Tapes

Audio tapes present stories with voice alone. Sometimes there may be a few sound effects. There is no audience and no body language to help create the image.

Listen for changes in the storyteller's voice. Does he or she use a different voice for each character? Does he or she speak loudly and softly? How does the speed of talking make you feel?

Long car rides are wonderful times to enjoy storytelling audio tapes. Later, you can take the tapes into your room and play them again and again to study how the storyteller uses voice to accomplish so many things.

Story Swapping

If you want to be a storyteller, you must tell stories. Look for every opportunity to tell a story. Sign up for workshops. Join a storytelling club. Have a storytelling party.

Tell your stories. Listen and trade. Are other storytellers—adults or children—telling a story you would like to use? Talk to them. Tell them you'd like to use it, too. Storytellers swap stories all the time. A story swap might be just a casual meeting with friends. It can be any of the places listed in Chapter 2, any place you tell or listen to a story. It can be an opportunity to collect a new idea.

Creating Story Collections

As you swap stories with other storytellers, you will build your own story collection. How do you keep a story collection? How do you organize it? How do you remember which story is which?

Some storytellers have a special box in which they keep written copies, notes, and tapes of their experiences. Some storytellers keep journals or scrapbooks of their storytelling adventures.

Many storytellers are very creative in how they advertise the stories they like and want to tell. One of these creative people decorated a sweatshirt with story symbols, one for each story. Another person painted story symbols on buttons which he wore on a hat. Another storyteller had a bracelet of storytelling charms. When

the collection became too long for a bracelet, she created a necklace.
Make storytelling collections as much fun as storytelling itself.

Videos To Watch

Here are some good videos that you may want to study.

Tell Me A Story, a collection of eight videos with storytellers Nancy
  Schimmel, Chuck Larkin, Michael "Badhair" Williams, and
  Beauty & the Beast Storytellers.

The Storytellers Collection, Atlas Video, Inc. 1991. Four videos with
  storytellers Olga Loya, Joe Bruchac, Alice McGill, and Jon
  Spelman.

Audio Tapes

There are many audio tapes for young people. They are all
collections of stories. Most are produced by a single storyteller.

A Storytelling Treasury, five cassettes recorded at the 20th Anniversary
  National Storytelling Festival, The National Storytelling Press.

Favorite Scary Stories of American Children, by Richard and July
  Dockrey Young.

Jack's First Job: and Other Appalaachian Jack Tales, by Donald Davis.

News from Lake Wobegon, by Garrison Keillor.

Sing Me A Story, by Heather Forest.

Tales To Grow On, by The Folktellers.

Traditional Tales for Children, by Donald Davis.

PART IV
Creating Storytelling Opportunities

CHAPTER 18

How To Hold
A Storytelling Party

★ **Is a big holiday coming soon?**
★ **Is it time for your birthday party?**
★ **Is your class planning to welcome a new kid?**

There are many reasons to have a party. Why not make it a story-telling party? You can have a storytelling party for any holiday, birthday, or special event.

The key to a successful party is in the planning. Take a little time in the beginning to carefully think about why you are having the party. Who will come? When and where you will have it? How long will it last? What will you do? What will you eat? Once you have the answer to these questions, you will be able to consider what things you will need and who can help you.

Why Have A Party?

It may be Halloween, Thanksgiving, or the Fourth of July. It may be your birthday. It may be the 100th birthday of your church or youth organization. Whatever your reason for having the party, you want it to be fun.

Select a theme that goes with your reason for having the party. It can be ghost tales for Halloween, science fiction for your birthday, or historical stories for an anniversary. Tie everything to this theme. The stories you tell, the crafts you make, the invitations and favors, costumes, even the food you eat should reflect the theme.

Some themes you could consider are

Friendship	Puppet Parade
Welcome	Crazy Characters
Ecology	Baseball
Circus	Basketball
Wildlife	Swimming
Pets	Model Mania

Use parties to experiment with storytelling. Try different things each time. What is most successful? What is most fun?

Who Will Come?

If the party is held in your class or youth group, the guest list will include everyone in that class or group. If it is a birthday or holiday party, look for family or friends that enjoy stories. Make a list of guests that get along well together.

If it is a private party at your home, you may want to limit the number of guests to three, five, or seven so that everyone gets a chance to participate.

When And Where Will It Be?

Will you have the party during or after school, in the evening, or on the weekend? What time will be best for you and the guests that you are inviting?

Where at school could it be held? Could it be at your house or in a community center? Is there a neighborhood park, beach, or camp where you can have a party? Is a church basement, barn, or empty garage available?

Think of possible places and then check with the adults who are in charge of those locations.

The place you choose could suggest a good theme. How could you decorate this place to carry out the theme and help create a mood for the storytelling?

How Long Will It Last?

Set a time and keep it short. Plan for an hour or an hour and a half. Do not let your party run over two hours. If you think you will need more time, have another party later. Let your friends leave while they are still having fun.

Long parties tend to run into problems. Allow just enough time to do the things you plan to do.

What Will You Do?

Plan activities for every moment. What will you do when kids begin to arrive? How will you keep them entertained until everyone gets there? Is there a game you can play or songs to sing?

Janice gave everyone a balloon when they arrived at her party. She also gave them markers to draw faces on the balloons. Later they used these balloon characters in a group story.

What activities will you do first, second, and last? How will you get the storytelling started?

You can use crafts to get the storytelling started. You could have kids watch a video or listen to a storyteller.

Be sure all these activities relate to the party theme.

What Will You Eat?

Will you have a campfire or barbecue? Will you make cookies or popcorn balls that have faces and become characters for stories? Can gingerbread boys be actors before they are eaten? Decorate ice cream cones and cake squares to coordinate with your theme.

What Things Will You Need?

Carefully plan for the things you will need before the party, such as invitations and room decorations. Make a list.

Then make another list of the things you will need during the party like food and favors.

When you have your lists finished, ask a parent, leader, or teacher to check them and make suggestions for additions.

Who Can Help You?

It's best to have an adult at the party. Parents, teachers, and youth group leaders often have good ideas to help your party run smoothly. Maybe you know a storyteller who could get things started or help guests learn to tell stories. It could be an adult or someone's older brother or sister.

What Kind Of Stories?

Choose stories that fit your theme and purpose. Or, you could choose a theme that fits the stories you like. What kind of stories do the guests like?

If your party is to welcome a new kid in class, youth group, or neighborhood, choose stories that will help that person learn about his or her new surroundings.

If the party is to celebrate a holiday, choose stories about that special day. If you are celebrating an anniversary, look for historical stories that explain the event.

You might want to suggest that each guest bring a story to share about the theme or purpose. Ask them to let you know in advance what they are planning so that you allow enough time in your scheduling.

Party Ideas

The kind of a party you have will suggest the theme. If it is your birthday, choose a theme from one of your favorite hobbies, sports or activities.

A Monster Magic Party

When Evan decided he wanted a storytelling birthday party, he chose monsters as a theme because he loved monsters and stories about them. His friends liked weird and scary monsters, but his little sister liked friendly ones. Evan liked any kind of monster.

Evan's house had a large basement where he and his sister could do messy crafts. When Evan thought his friends would like to make monster masks or costumes, he and his mother decided the basement would be a good place for the party.

Evan had three very good friends at school, one neighborhood buddy, a cousin about his age, and two pals from swim class. He wanted to invite them all.

Since some of the kids had parents who worked and couldn't get them to his house until after supper, Evan had to settle for an early evening party. He drew monster invitations with the time, date, and his address. Then he mailed them all.

Evan's mother saved old paper grocery sacks for the monster masks. Evan tried one on over his head. His mother marked where his eyes needed holes and where to cut out for his arms. Then he took off the sack and she cut the holes. He tried it on again. It was perfect.

It was Evan's job to assemble all the goodies to make the masks. He collected buttons, yarn, and fabric scraps. He found old bottles of glue and boxes of crayons. He spent a week begging recyclable odds and ends from neighbors, friends, aunts, uncles, and grandparents until he had a big box full.

Evan wanted each of his guests to make a monster mask. As they made it, he wanted them to make up things about this new monster. When they were finished, they would each wear their mask and tell a story about the monster.

Evan went to the library and collected all the monster stories he could find. He read them all and selected two for his mother to read at his party.

112

The day before his party, Evan went to his grandmother's house to make monster cookies. He decorated each one in a different way.

Evan decided that planning the party was as much fun as the party itself.

Stories Past

When Greg's class studied local history, he found some really good stories about their town from his great grandfather and other residents of a retirement home. When he told his teacher, his class decided to have a storytelling party at the retirement home to collect more stories.

"To get a good story, you have to give one away," his teacher told him. So Greg and two friends each found a story and practiced telling it.

The retirement home was delighted with the idea and offered to provide the refreshments.

Greg and his friends told their stories, which reminded many of the residents of some history that is not in any textbook.

The Teddy Bear Party

While Leslie was collecting stuffed toys for tots at Christmas, she decided it would be nice if her club did more than just give the toys to the kids. So she planned a storytelling party for the preschool group that was scheduled to receive the gifts. Each club member created a story to go with the toy.

At the preschool, the children were divided into small groups to hear the stories and receive the gifts. Some of the preschoolers were so excited they continued to make up stories about their animals.

Handicap Helpers

When one of his classmates was injured and needed to spend several months in a wheelchair, Doug thought a storytelling party might a way to help his classmate. It might also educate the whole class on how to offer useful help.

Doug contacted kids who either were currently in wheelchairs or who had spent some time in one. He asked them each to tell a story about the most helpful thing anyone had done for them. They could also tell stories that included other helpful hints.

Then Doug arranged for the school auditorium for this special party because it was wheelchair accessible.

Welcome Party

When a new classmate came to Jodi's room, she decided it would be a good idea to have a welcome party. She offered the services of her storytelling club. Each member, she told the teacher, could tell the new classmate a story about some activity at school or in the neighborhood. Her teacher liked the idea and suggested that some other classmates might like to join in the fun.

Mime Party

Because the kids in Ginny's workshop were not using enough hand, facial, and body movements, their storytelling coach suggested having a mime party. All the boys and girls painted their faces with black and white paint. They then drew stories out of a hat and had to tell them without using any words. They could only use hand, facial, and body movements. After each story the audience got to tell the story to see how good a mime each person was.

114

Family Parties

When Shelby found an old family photo album she couldn't wait until the next family gathering. Some of the photos were just people staring at the camera, but others were quite interesting and she was sure there were some good stories. Some pictures were of babies and little children, and she wondered who they were and what they were like. She wrote letters to family members and asked them to bring more pictures.

After the party, Shelby tried to write down as many things as she could remember in a storytelling journal.

For Further Reading

If you would like more ideas on holding parties with themes, you might want to look through the following books.

Children's Parties, by Judy Williams, Smithmark Publishers, 1992.
Great Theme Parties for Children, by Irene N. Watts, Sterling Publishing Co., 1991.

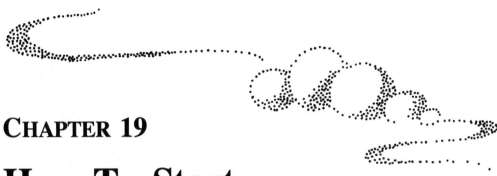

CHAPTER 19

How To Start
A Storytelling Club

★ **Do you enjoy storytelling parties?**
★ **Did you learn to tell stories in a workshop?**
★ **Would you like to swap stories with other kids?**

You can start a storytelling club. It can be as simple as a few friends meeting on your front porch on Thursday afternoon to share jokes and stories. It can be every Friday during lunch at school and anyone is welcome. Or, it can be at seven o'clock on the first Tuesday of every month at the community center with a local storyteller.

Some storytelling clubs meet at school. After a storytelling workshop in her classroom, Marla and four of her friends started a lunch-time club. Once a week they share stories during lunch. There are eight kids in the club and they take turns telling stories.

Some clubs are spin-offs of youth groups. After a few kids in Randy's 4-H club shared horseshowing experiences, their leader decided that these stories could help kids learn. So before the fair that year, his club exchanged tales about the do's and don'ts of the show ring. When kids began staying after closing to swap additional stories, storytime became a final windup to their monthly meetings.

Boys and girls who like horses, dogs, cats, baseball, soccer, camping, mysteries, fantasy, space or science enjoy sharing tales at club meetings. Some clubs are just informal gatherings on someone's front or back porch with soft drinks and popcorn.

No matter what kind of club you want to start, you need to take a few minutes to think about it and make some plans. Here are some questions to help you with your planning. Read them, think about them, and then make some lists to answer them.

Why are you starting the club?

Make a list of all the reasons you can think of. Why you want a club will determine what you will do in the club and who will join. It may help you to answer all the planning questions.

> to have fun
> to share stories
> to share tips and tricks
> to get ideas for new stories
> to get ideas for props and costumes
> to have a place to practice storytelling
> to make friends with other storytellers
> to do things as a group that you cannot do alone

Who will come to the meetings?

Will you have a limited number of members? Who will they be? You should include enough kids to be able to have a meeting if a few members are absent. However, it should not be so large that everyone cannot participate at every meeting.

If there is a lot of interest and too many kids want to join, have one large monthly meeting for everyone, and also have smaller groups that meet weekly. The large group may be able to plan some very special projects, and the smaller groups can maintain a cozy feeling.

Who else, in addition to members, could be included?

Any kids who want to come
Adult storytellers
Adult helpers
Special guests

How will you add new members?

Who can help you?

Where can you look for help to get your club started? Who might be able to stand by at meetings to help if there are problems?

Talk to the adults around you, especially those who work with children or youth activities. You may be surprised by how many people are not only interested in your ideas but who are also willing to help. Consider the following people.

Parents and other family members
Teachers

119

Youth group leaders
Religious leaders
Community organizations

What will you do at meetings?

What you do at your meetings will depend on why you are starting the club and who will come to the meetings. Here are some possible ideas you might want to consider.

Just talk, tell jokes and stories
Have guest storytellers
Take trips to storytelling festivals
Take trips for storytelling ideas
Hold storytelling parties
Put on your own storytelling festival
Learn how to tell better stories
Watch storytelling videos
Practice new ideas
Create puppets and props
Record stories on audio and video tapes

When will you meet?

When you meet might depend on who is included and what time is convenient for everyone.

During the school day
After school
In the evening
On weekends

120

Where will you meet?

Where you meet might also depend on who is included.

> At one member's home
> At a storyteller's home
> At school
> In a local church
> In a community center
> In a park

How will you conduct the meetings?

Establish some ground rules. You may have to go back and see how you answered the first five questions before you begin.

Opening

Plan to have everyone share something when they first come. Allow time for conversation. Do you want to play a game or light a storytelling candle?

Storytime

How will you decide who will tell what story and when? You may need to have some time limits so nobody hogs the stage.

Closing

Will you have some ritual for closing. Or will there be a snack time at the end?

121

Take the answers you have given to these questions and pretend you are at a typical meeting. What will happen first, second, third, last. When you think you will need something, have a problem, or cannot think of what will happen, make a note of it. Ask your parents or teachers or friends for advice.

Do not have too many rules at first. Rules are usually created to solve problems and may not be needed in your club.

You might want to kick off your club with a storytelling party as the first meeting or as a way to get interested kids together. A club can also form after a workshop or festival to allow participants to continue the storytelling fun.

Hold An Organizational Meeting

When you have carefully thought out your plans, you are ready to have an organizational meeting. This means getting all the kids together, going over your ideas, and deciding what everyone wants to do. When everyone helps form the club they are more enthusiastic about it.

You can begin an organizational meeting by,

1. Asking why members want to join the club. This will help you plan meetings and activities that the members will enjoy.

2. Asking members what they want to do. Bring out your lists of suggestions and put all the possibilities to a vote.

3. Discussing ground rules that would make everyone more comfortable. You may want to use many of the suggestions

given below under "What To Expect From Members."

4. Asking members to consider three questions before next meeting. What can the group do for them? What can it do for the community? What can they do for the group?

Select A Name For Your Club
Although you could select a name for your club at the organizational meeting, it is best to let members think about it for a few days to come up with the best ideas. You can present the idea and some suggestions at the first meeting and then vote on it later.
Some suggestions that others have used are,

> Junior Storytellers (Could add name of town, school, church or organization, such as Westbrook Junior Storytellers)
> Junior Folktellers
> Kid Taletellers
> Tale Spinners or Talespinners
> Spellbinders
> Storykids
> Storyteens
> Story Weavers or Storyweavers
> Young Yarnspinners

What To Expect From Members
Everyone will enjoy club meetings and activities more if you let all kids know at the beginning that membership in this club requires

some commitments from them. Some requirements for good members that other clubs have used are,

> Good members come to meetings on time
> Good members listen to stories
> Good members volunteer to tell stories
> Good members volunteer to help organize events
> Good members give helpful, positive comments
> Good members respect the ideas of others
> Good members accept changes when needed
> Good members are enthusiastic about group activities
> Good members compliment others when they have done a good
> job of storytelling, planning, or providing refreshments

Choose Some Officers

Even though your club is just a few kids that meet once a week on your front porch, it will help if someone is in charge. That person can make sure the club continues to meet, and helps gets it started and ended on time. If your club is a larger or more organized one, you may need additional officers.

There are three ways you can select your officers.

1. Rotate the job. Select a system, such as alphabetically according to the first letter in the person's last name. Begin with A or Z and have each kid serve as officer for three months, six months, or a year. No longer. It's important to give everyone a chance. Kids who have held an office are more understanding of others.

2. Elect officers. You can decide on what officers you need. Ask for nominations and then elect them. Although this is the democratic way, it tends to put popular kids in office and often hurts less popular but talented members.

3. Appoint and approve a slate of officers. This method usually selects the most qualified people and those most willing to offer their services. Many organizations use this method. It gives a nominating committee or adult leader an opportunity to discuss the job with the nominee.

Some officers you may want to have in your club are,

President, director, or manager. Call it any name, but this person is in charge. It should be someone who is responsible and can take a leadership position.

Program chairman. This person will arrange activities for meetings and special events. You can always appoint others to help with large projects.

Refreshment chairman. This person is responsible for seeing that there are snacks at every meeting. He or she does not have to provide them each time. A refreshment chairman may have a list of volunteers and remind them when their turn comes.

Secretary. Even if you do not want to record all the proceedings of informal meetings, it is a good idea to keep a record

125

of who tells what story when. You may need to go back over such records when you plan a concert or if someone requests a storyteller from your group.

Treasurer. You may only need a treasurer for special events and you can choose one at that time. Look for someone who is honest and good at math.

Establish A Club Identity

Many club members are proud of their club and like to feel that they belong. Sometimes it helps to promote this group spirit.

At one of your first meetings you can make a club banner to hang in your meeting place during meetings. It should have the club name on it and any other decorations or symbols that you want. It could list all of the members names.

You could also make some club T-shirts or sweatshirts with the club name and the member name. You can get fabric paint and ideas at any craft or fabric store.

Talk About Money

One of the joys of storytelling is that it is an activity that does not require money. You can meet and enjoy stories for no cost at all.

If your group wants to do some special things, however, you might need some cash. The club may want to collect dues, but that is not a wise idea. Money in a treasury is a temptation. When you need money you can ask for donations or earn what you need.

Some ways to get money are often more fun than the project you are trying to sponsor.

126

Get Donations

When you need money for a special project, you can start with your parents. Can you ask each member to contribute?

If you need more money than you can gather from members, look to your community. Some organizations sponsor club activities for young people and your project may qualify.

If you need specific things, you might try to collect used items. When one club needed costumes, they held a drive shortly after Halloween for outgrown items. They received so many that they used what they could and then had a garage sale before Halloween the next year. Another group did the same thing to collect puppets.

Barter For Your Needs

Barter means trade. You trade something you have and do not need for something someone else has that you do need.

What do you have that you could trade? Costumes? Puppets? Stories?

Remember the story of "The Storytelling Stone" in Chapter 7? At the end the orphan boy traded stories for food and clothing. How can you trade your stories?

Earn The Money

Earning money and bartering may involve the same projects. The only difference is how you are paid. When you barter you get something in trade. When you receive money as payment, you are earning it.

Look through the list of special projects, or make up your own list, to see if there is something you can do to earn money.

How To Plan Activities

When you are asked to plan the activities for your club, you may think that there is no way you will be able to think of enough things for every meeting. But there is a magic way to plan that will give you so many ideas you will be struggling to fit them all in.

That magic way is advance planning. Take a calendar and begin planning for your entire term in office.

Special holidays

Mark the special holidays that occur in these months. Can you plan something on the meetings just before the holidays to help celebrate them? Can you plan a bigger project for the occasion?

School days off

Are there any days, such as teacher inservice days, when you and your club members do not have school? Can you plan a trip or activity to take advantage of these special days.

Community events

Mark the dates for special community events such as County Fair, Fourth of July, or Winter Festival. Check with your Chamber of Commerce, City Hall, or Community Center for information on events to include. Find out if your club can participate in some of them. Allow enough time in your planning to practice and prepare stories for these events.

Storytelling festivals

Are there any storytelling festivals that are planned for your area? Will there be kid workshops included in them? Check with adult storytelling groups in your area. They will be good helpers for a lot of things you plan to do. If your local library, newspaper, and Chamber of Commerce do not know of any local storytelling groups, you may want to write to the national organization for information. The address for The National Association for the Preservation and Perpetuation of Storytelling (NAPPS) is P.O. Box 309, Jonesborough, Tennessee 37659.

Museums

Check with local museums to see if they are planning any special activities or programs. Find out if your club could prepare and tell stories about the items in the museum as part of their program.

All Around Town

Check with parks, preschools, businesses, and associations. Who could use some storytellers? You might even find some way to earn some money for your services.

Other Schools and Storytellers

Is there a teacher who is planning a storytelling unit for her classroom who could use your help or your stories? Could adult storytellers use your help to make props? Offering the services of your club members can uncover some very interesting activities.

Additional Activities

If you need some fill-in activities for a meeting or two between special projects, you could watch videos or listen to audio tapes of storytellers. You could have everyone create a craft, such as a sock puppet that could be used in a story. You can choose a theme for the next meeting and have everyone bring a story on that theme.

Plan an event that can be held anytime. Arrange a campfire storytelling trip to a local or state park. Invite a storyteller to visit your club.

If you've scheduled all these ideas on your calendar, you may already have a pretty full program planned. Talk over these ideas with all the club members. They may know of more events that you have not yet included.

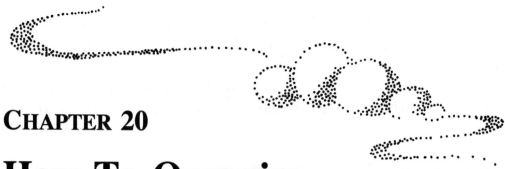

CHAPTER 20

How To Organize
A Young Storytellers Festival

★ **Were you in a storytelling project at school?**
★ **Were you in a storytelling workshop at a community center?**
★ **Does your club want to show off its storytelling talent?**

You are now ready to put on a show, a concert, a performance for younger kids or parents and friends.

A festival is often held at the end of a school project or workshop. It's like a band or choral concert at the end of the school year. Only this concert features stories instead of music.

This is not a contest! If you are competing for ribbons, awards, or prizes, that is the main thing you think about. And your joy is in the reward.

In a concert all of the pieces are enjoyed and appreciated. People come to a concert to hear the music or the stories. Make this your main reason for holding a festival. Let the audience enjoy and appreciate all of the stories. Storytelling should be fun. It is a sharing time.

Since it is a concert, you prepare for it the same way you plan a musical program. Here are some questions to help you plan your festival.

When will you hold your festival?

What is the day, date and time of your program? If the festival is at the end of a school project or workshop, it should be scheduled as a last meeting or an evening soon after the final session. If it is a stand-alone event, allow enough time for storytellers to prepare their stories and people to plan to attend. Several weeks or months might be needed. Giving yourself enough time for all the details will make the job a lot easier.

One 4-H club chose a time shortly before fair. The prepared an evening of storytelling about their experiences showing at fairs. They presented it to younger, new members who had never shown before.

Some small towns have special events like Pumpkin Pie Day, The Strawberry Festival, or a Corn Roast. You might prepare a storytelling festival to add to the activities at one of your town's gatherings.

Where will you hold the festival?

Will your festival be in the school auditorium, a meeting room at a community center, or at a park? Sometimes storytelling festivals are held at museums or historical places as part of another celebration or event.

Look for opportunities to hold mini-festivals, too. Instead of an evening or afternoon function with many storytellers, a mini-festival might have one two or three performers. These shorter festivals are great entertainment to feature after a luncheon, banquet, or as part of a conference. You might take stories you have already prepared, or design a program specially for an organization or business.

Why are you holding this festival?

Your festival may be a finale to a workshop or study project, but there are many other opportunities. Holiday celebrations, tourist attractions, and religious gatherings can all offer storytellers a stage.

One youth organization used members who were storytellers to tell original stories for their recruitment night program. Once a year this group invited kids who were interested in joining and their parents to come and learn more about the organization. Each storyteller told about activities that they experienced.

Who will be the storytellers?

All the participants in a workshop or class project should have a chance to tell their stories. If your event will be open, you may have to have tryouts. If you are holding it together with another event, such as a banquet of businessmen, you might want to select kids who have appropriate stories for this audience.

How many stories should you include?

How many stories you need may depend on the length of the stories or the time that is available. If you are giving an afternoon festival, an hour might be all the time that is available. If you are

133

giving an evening performance, have an auditorium reserved, and can plan on an intermission, you can schedule a two-hour program.

If you are telling stories to young children, do not plan to tell more than two or three. Keep the program to about twenty minutes.

How will you arrange the program?

As you set up the program, you will need to consider who goes first, last, and in the middle. The first storyteller needs to be good to get the program going. It should be a lively happy story instead of a slow sad one. The tellers who are last are usually your best, ones that are hard for other people to follow. In the middle, alternate strong and weak ones, slow and fast, happy and sad. You may need to also consider the order according to theme or length of story. Don't put two long ones together. Put a short one in between.

Prepare a printed program for your audience.

Storytellers like to see their name in print. The audience likes to be able to follow the listing. Your program can be a simple list of the storytellers, the name of the story they will tell, and the order in which they will appear. See the sample program on page 141.

If you have room in your program, it would be nice to tell something about the storyteller and the story.

How will you get people to come?

If your storytelling concert is part of another event, someone else may be responsible for advertising. If you are doing this yourself with a club, you may need to do your own advertising. Take as much time preparing your advertising as you take to prepare your program.

Prepare a flyer.

You can let a lot of people know about your program with a flyer. Make one 8.5 x 11-inch sign and photocopy 100 copies or more. You can make the original on your computer, like the sample on page 142, or draw and hand-letter it any way you want.

Be sure your flyer has all the important information.

Name of the festival
Time and date
Location
Price of ticket
Phone number to call for more information

If you have room, any additional information is helpful and can convince readers to attend.

Who is sponsoring it
Who the storytellers will be
Why it is being held (if it is a fundraiser)

Post your flyer all over town.

Now think of all the possible places you could put your flyer. Some ideas to begin with are,

Bulletin boards at school
Bulletin boards at community centers
In store windows
Library bulletin boards

You may want to give friends and family a handful of flyers to distribute to people who might be interested.

You might be able to place a pile of flyers on a desk in an office or bank.

Can you mail some flyers to other schools, youth groups, teams, or churches.

Who would be interested in coming to your festival? How can you get flyers to these people?

Can you get information in a newspaper?

You might want to send one of your flyers to the local newspaper. You could also call them on the phone to see if they would like to do an article about your project and maybe take a photograph. Some small town and some community newspapers are interested in these kind of articles. Large city newspapers often are not. It is worth trying, however, because a lot of people read these newspapers.

Can you get information in newsletters?

Newsletters are also a wonderful way to reach a lot of people who might want to come to your festival. If your storytelling club is part of a larger organization, find out if they have a newsletter. If you are putting on this festival with another organization, do they have a newsletter?

Check at school and the public library for other newsletters that may be interested in your project.

Allow plenty of time to get information to newsletters, because many are published quarterly or bimonthly.

Will there be a parade in your town?

If your festival is part of a county fair or community event, there may be a parade as part of the ceremonies. A float in the parade could be a fun way to advertise your festival.

Even if you do not have a festival planned, consider entering your club in local parades. It makes your community aware of you and may lead to some requests for performances in the future.

Prepare some signs and banners for showtime.

If you are at a school, fair, museum, or other large location, how will people know where to find you?

Make some large signs or banners to direct people to the right room or building. Tape the signs on the wall or put them on sticks that can be pushed into the ground. You may want to get permission to place these.

If you cannot get permission to place signs, have one of your members, dressed in costume, at an entrance to give directions.

Create a festival workshop.

Because storytelling is becoming so very popular, many more workshops are now available for young people. Some schools, youth groups, churches, and camps are even sponsoring a new kind of workshop, a festival workshop, to get boys and girls interested in storytelling.

While concert festivals are performed at the end of a study unit, these new festival workshops are presented at the beginning of a project. They are organized more like conferences and help young people explore the many opportunities available in storytelling.

137

A Story Circus

The Story Circus is a district-wide festival workshop for middle school boys and girls to present different kinds of storytelling. Many storytellers come to teach one-hour sessions about their own styles and methods. Each session is scheduled in a different room. Although several sessions are taught at the same time, many are repeated. Boys and girls are given programs in advance so that they may choose the classes they wish to attend.

Different kinds of stories are usually offered, including myth, fairy tale, legends, mystery, science fiction, history, adventure, and personal experience. Different methods often include dramatic telling, singing with instruments, drawing and cutting, and dancing. Some storytellers use puppets, props, and costumes.

Storytelling Crafts Festival Workshop

When some junior storytellers wanted to explore their options for using crafts for storytelling, they asked their leaders for help. What started as a small workshop by some local artists and craftsmen grew to become a craft festival workshop. Many people in the area volunteered their time to come help the young people learn how to make a variety of puppets, masks, costumes, drums, bells, and other items to use with their stories.

Explore different kinds of storytelling.

To encourage young people to explore the many different kinds of stories and storytelling, one director opened a story circus with an adaptation of the tale of the five blind men and the elephant.

The Five Blind Men And The Elephant

Many years ago, in a far-away country, five blind men wanted to see what an elephant looked like.

One day a friend took them to meet one.

The first blind man walked to the elephant, reached out, and touched its trunk. "Oh," he said. "An elephant is like a fat snake."

The second blind man walked up to the elephant, reached out, and touched its tusk. "Oh, no," he said. "An elephant has a hard shell like a turtle."

While the first two were arguing, the third blind man walked up to the elephant, reached out, and touched its ear. "Oh, no," he said. "An elephant is flat like a bird's wing."

While the first three were arguing, the fourth blind man walked to the rear or the elephant. When he reached out, he touched its tail. "Oh, no," he said. "An elephant is like a skinny stick."

While the other four were arguing, the fifth blind man walked to the elephant. He reached out and touched its side. "Oh, my," he said. "It's much bigger, it's so much more."

Then the fifth blind man touched the elephant's ear, ran his hand down the animal's trunk, and felt its tusk. Without waiting to touch the tail, he said, "Yes, my friends, it is as you say. It is like a fat snake, a turtle shell, a bird's wing, and a skinny stick. But it is also *very much more!*

139

Storytelling is a lot like this elephant. There are many different kinds of stories and many different ways of telling them. Storytelling is all of it. And it is also *very much more!*

Explore all of it. There is a special place waiting for you.

Share A Story
Folktales From Around The World

The Three Sillies
From A Mexican Folktale
BY MARTA MARTINEZ

The Wise Woman
From A Polish Folktale
BY TOM KOLINSKI

Lazy Jack
From An English Folktale
BY TEDDY HILL

Stone Soup
From A Scandinavian Story
BY JODY JOHNSON

Intermission

A Little Old Lady And A Leprechaun
From An Irish Folktale
BY ERIN O'CONNELL

Vassilissa The Beautiful
From A Russian Folktale
BY IVAN ROMONOF

INDEX

Please send me information on:

___ **Workbooks for Storytelling Workshops**
___ **Discounts on bulk purchases for workshops and classes**
___ **Special prices for multiple copies for storytelling clubs and youth organizations**

Let me know when new books are published about:

___ **Stories For Children To Tell**
___ **Stories About Young Storytellers**

Name_____

Address_____

City_____State_____Zip_____

STORYCRAFT PUBLISHING
P.O. BOX 205
MASONVILLE, CO 80541-0205

Want to know more about:

- ★ **Other Kid Storytellers**
- ★ **Stories To Tell**
- ★ **Storytelling Crafts To Make**
- ★ **Ideas For Storytelling Parties**
- ★ **Activities For Storytelling Clubs**

Send for information about subscribing to *The Junior Storyteller*, an exciting newsletter for young storytellers. Find out what other kids are doing. Discover new ideas to use with your stories. Learn about storytelling activities for kids.

Special subscription rates are available for:
Storytelling Clubs, Schools, Libraries, Youth Organizations

Storycraft Publishing, P.O. Box 205, Masonville, CO 80541-0205

Please send me information on how I can get a subscription to:

The Junior Storyteller

Name_____

Address_____

City_____State_____Zip_____

Mail to: Storycraft Publishing, P.O. Box 205, Masonville, CO 80541-0205